TRIADS FOR THE IMPROVISING GUITARIST

JANE MILLER

To access audio visit:
www.halleonard.com/mylibrary
Enter Code
6822-1792-9157-2744

RECORDING

Jane Miller, Guitar
Mike Kelly, Bass
Steve Chaggaris, Drums
Tom Eaton, Recording, Mixing, and Mastering at Universal Noise Storage, Newburyport, MA

BERKLEE PRESS

Editor in Chief: Jonathan Feist
Senior Vice President of Online Learning and Continuing Education/CEO of Berklee Online: Debbie Cavalier
Vice President of Enrollment Marketing and Management: Mike King
Vice President of Academic Strategy: Carin Nuernberg
Editorial Assistants: Zach Green, Emily Jones, and Brittany McCorriston

ISBN 978-0-87639-202-7

Study music online at
online.berklee.edu

DISTRIBUTED BY

7777 W. BLUEMOUND RD. P.O. BOX 13819
MILWAUKEE, WISCONSIN 53213

Visit Hal Leonard Online
www.halleonard.com

1140 Boylston Street
Boston, MA 02215-3693 USA
(617) 747-2146

Visit Berklee Press Online at
www.berkleepress.com

Berklee Press, a publishing activity of Berklee College of Music, is a not-for-profit educational publisher.
Available proceeds from the sales of our products are contributed to the scholarship funds of the college.

Copyright © 2020 Berklee Press.
All Rights Reserved

No part of this publication may be reproduced in any form or by any means without the prior written permission of the Publisher.

CONTENTS

ACKNOWLEDGMENTS iv

INTRODUCTION vi

PART I. BASIC TRIADS 1

    Chapter 1. Major Triads 3

    Chapter 2. Minor Triads 8

    Chapter 3. Diminished Triads 10

    Chapter 4. Augmented Triads 13

    Chapter 5. The Triads, Organized 15

PART II. LARGER CHORDS AND TRIADS 16

    Chapter 6. Major 7 Chords and Their Matched Minor Triads 17

    Chapter 7. Minor 7 Chords and Their Matched Major Triads 24

    Chapter 8. Dominant 7 Chords Matched with Diminished Triads 28

    Chapter 9. Minor 7♭5 Chords 33

    Chapter 10. Diminished 7 Chords 37

    Chapter 11. Minor-Major 7 Chords 41

    Chapter 12. Matches and Deals: A Recap 45

    Chapter 13. Extensions and Natural Tensions 47

    Chapter 14. Altered Tensions 49

PART III. COMPING AND SOLOING 51

    Chapter 15. Comping 53

    Chapter 16. Soloing 66

ABOUT THE AUTHOR 69

ACKNOWLEDGMENTS

The students in my Visualizing Chords lab at Berklee College of Music have been helpful sounding boards, mirrors, fellow experimenters, and deep thinkers as they fix their gazes on my scribbles on the board before them. Our classroom truly becomes a lab as we try this material out—guitars in hands—in pairs, in larger groups, in the round, and in our minds' ears as we verbally kick things around. They, along with my private guitar students, have guided and pushed me toward the dark corners of my thought process about the material in this book, helping me to illuminate and articulate what I had only been using abstractly on my own. It made sense to me. The challenge was to bring it to the point of making sense to others. My students have my gratitude and respect. Thank you to Kim Perlak, chair of the Guitar Department at Berklee, for allowing me the chance and the freedom to develop the course.

Playing with other musicians and talking about what we do is a sure beginning of a growth spurt. I appreciate all of the engaging and creative musicians I've worked with over the years, and I thank you all collectively. Special thanks must go to Eric Skye for the inspiring hangs and time with our guitars. My friend saxophonist Cercie Miller saw me through many duo gigs during which I learned a lot about comping, and I'm grateful for that. David Clark has been a solid bass player, challenging composer, and relatable musician to me. Bassist and guitarist-singer-songwriter Mike Kelly's contagious enthusiasm and creative musical moments with me are as valuable as his help when I've needed rides. Mike, drummer Stephan Chaggaris, and engineer Tom Eaton made quick and easy professional work of the audio recordings for this book. Pianist Tim Ray manages to read my composer mind with ease, which puts me at ease while inspiring me to do something interesting. Tim, Lincoln Goines on bass, and Mark Walker on drums gave me the gift of their high-level musicianship while recording my album *Boats*. Singer-songwriter and friend Sonia Rutstein invited me to play with her on shows and recordings over twenty years ago. I tried out a lot of this material then, showing myself the stylistic diversity of the concept.

My travel enablers from Berklee include Damien Bracken, Jason Camelio, and Alexia Rosari, who provided and encouraged opportunities to present much of the material found here in clinics and master classes worldwide. I am humbled and grateful to them all.

Zach Green stepped up and transformed himself from a former hard-working student of mine to a valuable hard-working notation and guitar diagram editor and interpreter. I knew that he would completely understand my thought process and scribbles, and I'm lucky and grateful for his work.

ACKNOWLEDGMENTS

Jonathan Feist has once again talked me through the process of writing a book. For our second effort, we had long phone conversations during which I would pace back and forth on my deck while my dog Betty did her own pacing in the yard wondering why we weren't taking longer walks. It's a funny thing, this identifying and naming an idea to turn into a book. I've relied on Jonathan's editorial expertise and business sense as much as I've relied on any musician I've worked with. Thanks for keeping the faith and for keeping an eye on things.

INTRODUCTION

"Tell me and I'll forget; show me and I may remember; involve me and I'll understand."
—Chinese Proverb

This book is full of shapes. You'll see some standard notation, too, but the heavy emphasis is on the visualization of chord shapes. While it may be a relief to be given the green light to use the shapes of chord forms as our tool for learning and memorizing, there will still be theory involved, and reading notation will be part of that. But, yes, you are hereby given permission to use shapes as your tools for the memorization of triads. It's how our brains work anyway, so fighting that process is frustrating and not as necessary as you may have been led to believe. Rather than abandoning the quest for learning notes all over the fretboard, however, you'll see that using visualization methods of learning chord forms around the neck will have the side benefit of reinforcing note locations. That will help your reading!

This book contains exercises that will help you to memorize the shapes of the triads in all of their inversions. Once those shapes become second nature, you'll see that identifying the highest note of each triad inversion will light the way for playing seventh chords (and beyond) in any key. Exercises in voice leading will become a springboard to creating melodies and improvising using the shapes as your guide. Using only the first three strings as a reference, the exercises will show you how to easily flow from one chord to another, whether in a solo or while comping.

We will begin with the basics of triadic theory, build to identifying triad matches with seventh chords, and finally create single-note lines over chord progressions. This book will encourage you to review, get a different perspective on how you see and use chords, and become better equipped to improvise over any set of changes.

The system that this book presents involves seeing the triads within seventh chords and larger structures. It allows for mixing in your already-in-use techniques and strategies for soloing. Integrate scales, arpeggios, quartal playing, your mind's ear—whatever is already working for you. Use this system when you want to play over changes reliably and need a place to start. When it's hard to get a grip on a tonal center for more than a fleeting couple of bars, visualizing triads (as this book illustrates) will add to your vocabulary and musical ideas. Your visual memory will feed you the information when you need it, your mind's ear will respond, and your hands will know what to do.

With practice.

ABOUT THE AUDIO

To access the accompanying audio, go to www.halleonard.com/mylibrary and enter the code found on the first page of this book. This will grant you instant access to every example. Examples with accompanying audio are marked with an audio icon.

PART I
Basic Triads

CHAPTER 1

Major Triads

Triads are three-note chords. *Major triads* consist of the interval of a major third from the root and a perfect fifth from the root. That creates a minor third between the third of the chord and the fifth. For example, a C major triad, spelled C-E-G, has a major third between the notes C and E, and a perfect fifth between C and G. That leaves a minor third between the notes E and G.

FIG. 1.1. C Major Triad and Its Intervals: Major third, Minor third, Perfect fifth

In any key, the triad that is built from the first degree of the major scale will be major: R 3 5 is the formula. Two other major triads naturally occur in any major scale: the chords built on the fourth and fifth scale degrees. See the F and G triads in figure 1.2.

FIG. 1.2. F and G Major Triads

F contains the interval of a major third between the notes F and A, and a minor third between the notes A and C. Again, there is a perfect fifth between the lowest and highest notes, F and C. This fits the description of a major triad, but without even analyzing the chord for intervals, you can quickly identify a major triad by seeing that it would be the first chord of its major scale. The notes F, A, and C are the first, third, and fifth notes of an F major scale. Similarly, the notes G, B, and D are the first, third, and fifth notes of a G major scale.

Major triads are known by their characteristically happy sound. Many guitarists learn a handful of major triads very early in their development and can get several simple songs up and running with them: "Skip to My Lou," "On Top of Old Smokey," etc. You'll recognize these chords, often referred to as "cowboy chords" or "campfire chords" because of their common use among acoustic guitarists at sing-alongs. These are all major triads. Using all six strings—or anything more than three strings—and you'll find some of the notes are doubled or tripled.

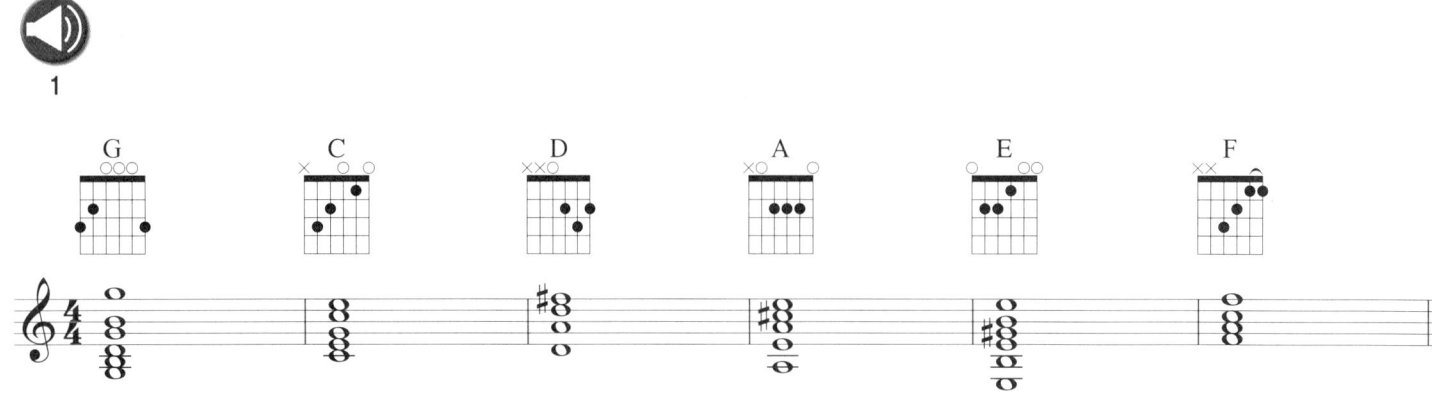

FIG. 1.3. Common Triad Forms

Add barre chords to this collection, and you'll see that the common forms for E and A major triads can be transposed by moving them up or down the neck following the root of the chord around on the sixth string or fifth string, referred to as Root 6 or Root 5.

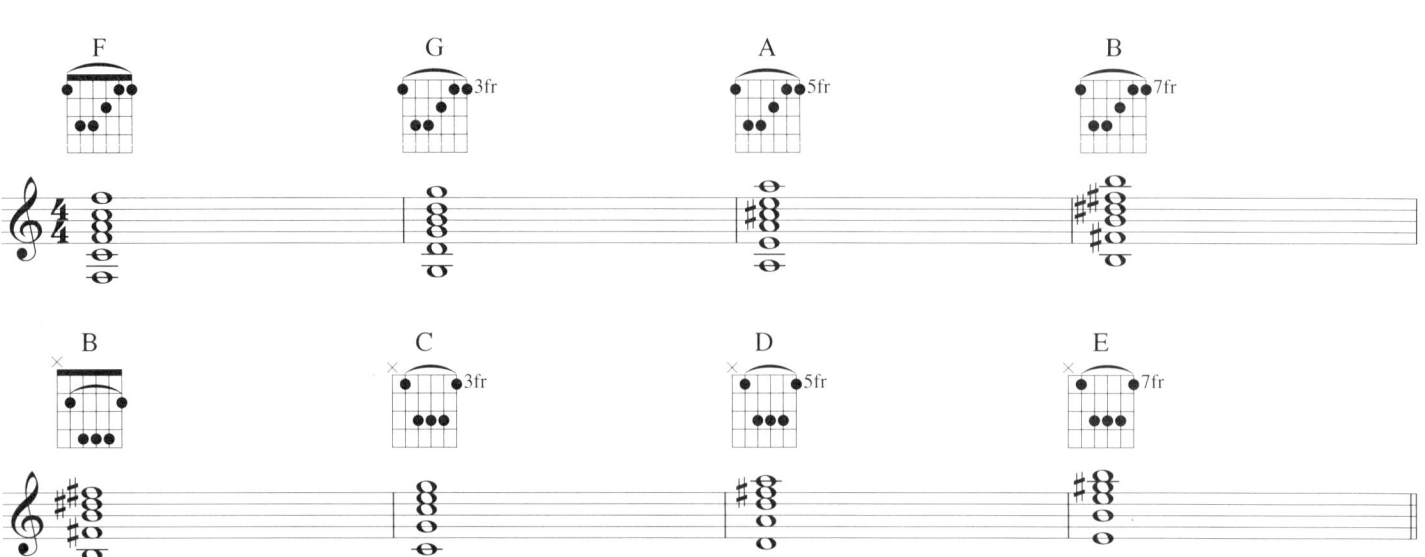

FIG. 1.4. Common Barre Chords, Root 6 and Root 5

If you zoom in to the first three strings of either of these major barre chord types, you'll see the three notes that make up the triad. This C barre chord at the third fret contains a C major triad on the first three strings.

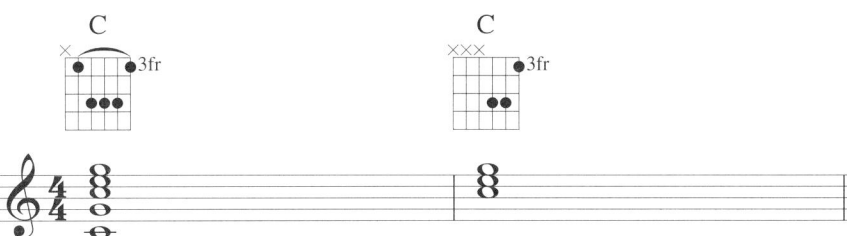

FIG. 1.5. C Barre Chord, C Triad

The F barre chord at the first fret contains the notes of an F major triad on the first three strings.

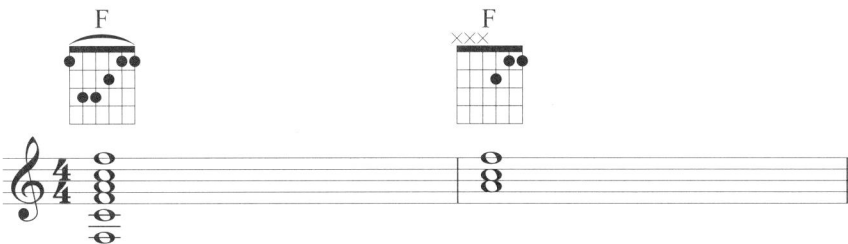

FIG. 1.6. F Barre Chord, F Triad

Inversions of triads refer to the order of the notes in the chord from low to high, including root position (as they occur in the scale), first inversion (third, fifth, and root of chord), and second inversion (fifth, root, and third of chord).

Here are the three inversions of an F major triad:

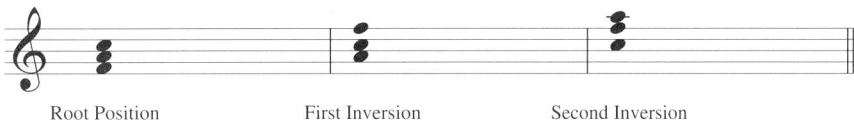

FIG. 1.7. F Root, First, Second Inversions

Notice that in figure 1.6, the F triad that is on the first three strings has the notes A C F, which is a first inversion F major triad. In figure 1.5, you see a C major triad from the root on the first three strings: C E G. That leaves second inversion for you to recognize in a familiar chord form.

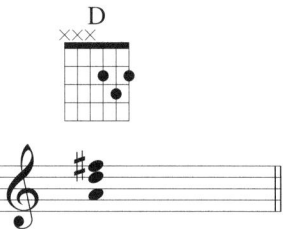

FIG. 1.8. D Second Inversion

Name the notes from low to high on this familiar D triad and see A, D, and F#. That is a second inversion triad since the fifth is in the lowest voice, followed by the root, and then the third on top.

You now have three different inversions of a major chord to use on the first three strings. Unlike their barre chord versions, these triads use only three strings with a different note of the chord on each string; very efficient. But, similar to barre chords, these chords are moveable.

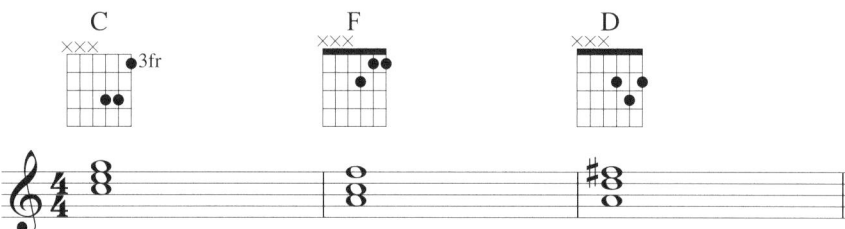

FIG. 1.9. C Root, F First Inversion, D Second Inversion

Identify the notes in each of these major triads as they appear in these chord forms. More importantly, identify how each note functions in the chord; in other words, name the chord tones R, 3, and 5. Pay special attention to the note that falls on the first (E) string. This will be useful information going forward. The answers are below:

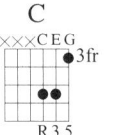  

FIG. 1.10. Chord Tones

Watch what happens as you move these triad forms up the neck. Take a D major triad up one whole step (two frets) and land on E major. Here's the good part: as you name the notes (B, E, G♯), you'll discover that the chord tones (5, R, 3) haven't changed from the second inversion D major.

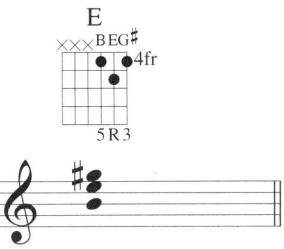

FIG. 1.11. E Major Triad Second Inversion

Go ahead and randomly move the major triads around the neck and identify the names and numbers. Here are a few possibilities:

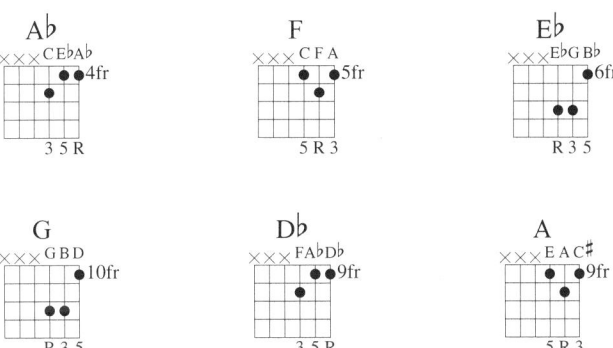

FIG. 1.12. Random Triad Inversions

Notice which note falls on the first string (E) on each root position triad (the fifth), each first inversion triad (the root), and each second inversion triad (the third). You can count on that phenomenon being consistent, which will help you find shortcuts as you navigate the fretboard with this system of following triad shapes using chord tone identification.

CHAPTER 2

Minor Triads

Minor triads contain the interval of a minor third starting on the root and a perfect fifth starting on the root. There is a major third between the third and fifth of the chord, just the opposite of the interval relationship in a major triad. The characteristic sound is "sad," as compared to the "happy" sounding major triads.

The formula for a minor triad is R♭3 5. Temporarily, think of the root of the chord as the first note of a major scale. Then flat the third note of that scale (lower it by one-half step), and add the fifth to create a minor triad. Or, more simply, flat the third of any major triad to get a minor triad. This could also be thought of as seeing the root third and fifth from a minor scale as a minor triad. Any major scale naturally contains three minor triads, said to be *diatonic* to the key: the IImi, IIImi, and VImi chords, or triads built on the second, third, and sixth scale degrees without altering any notes in the scale. In the key of C, the three diatonic minor triads are Dmi (D F A), Emi (E G B), and Ami (A C E).

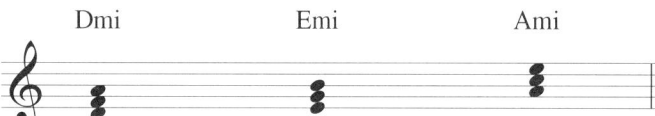

FIG. 2.1. Dmi, Emi, and Ami Triads

Here are a few familiar minor triad chord forms:

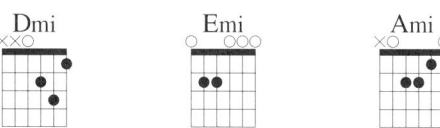

FIG. 2.2. Common Minor Triad Forms

CHAPTER 2. Minor Triads (Miller)

Using the major triad forms on the first three strings from chapter 1, you can make minor triads once you have identified which note is the third of the chord. C from the root becomes Cmi by lowering the E on the second string by one fret, or one-half step, to get to E♭. The first inversion F major triad becomes Fmi by lowering the A on the third string to A♭. The second inversion D major turns to Dmi by lowering the F♯ on the first string to F natural.

8

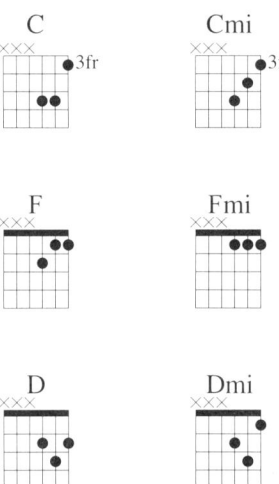

FIG. 2.3. Three-String Minor Triad Forms

As you did in chapter 1, identify which chord tone is on the high E string for your reference point in maneuvering around the neck. True to their major counterparts, the minor triads have the following high notes on the first string:

- Cmi root: G
- Fmi first inversion: F
- Dmi second inversion: F.

That is the fifth, the root, and the flat third, respectively.

Go ahead and move those minor triads around the fretboard randomly, and identify the notes and chord tones that fall on the first string.

Here are some examples:

9

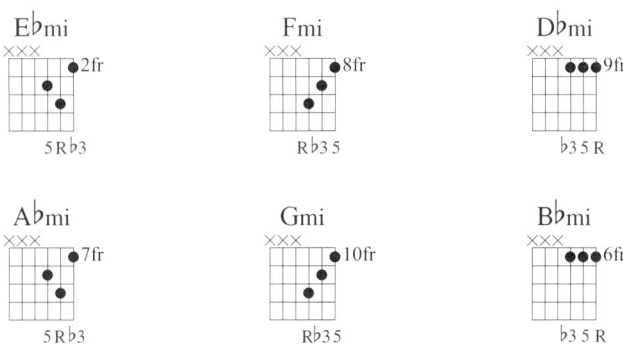

FIG. 2.4. Random Minor Triads with their Chord Tones

CHAPTER 3

Diminished Triads

Diminished triads contain two minor third intervals and a diminished fifth interval from the root to the fifth of the chord. The formula for diminished triads is R ♭3 ♭5. One diminished triad occurs diatonically in a major scale: the triad built from the seventh degree of a major scale (B from a C major scale) is a diminished triad, shown in figure 3.1.

FIG. 3.1. B° Triad

The notes B D F spell a diminished triad, fitting the formula of R ♭3 ♭5. Using a B major scale as a reference to the chord construction, you'll see that D and F are both sharp in the key of B, making D and F natural the flat 3 and flat 5, respectively.

While diminished 7 chords are more commonly used in popular music and jazz, we will make good use of diminished triads and their higher purpose throughout this book.

Here are some forms for playing diminished triads using only three strings at a time:

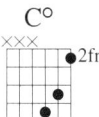 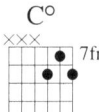 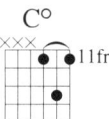

FIG. 3.2. Diminished Triad Forms on the First Three Strings

The sound of diminished chords is notably full of tension. As an exercise to get quick at these chord forms and to get your ears involved in their distinctive sound, practice these examples in resolving the B° to the C triads in figure 3.3.

CHAPTER 3. Diminished Triads (Miller)

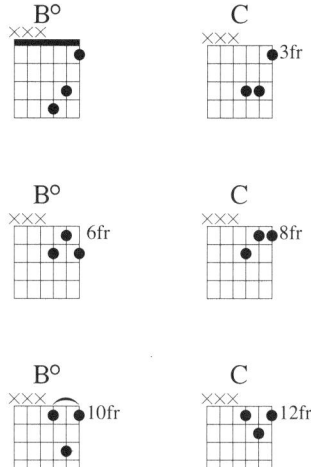

FIG. 3.3. B° to C

Focus again on the first three strings and make a note of which chord tone falls on the first string of each inversion of a diminished triad. B° from the root has F or ♭5 as the high note, B° first inversion has B or root on top, and B° second inversion has D or ♭3 on top.

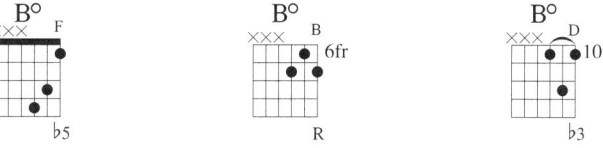

FIG. 3.4. Notes on Top of B° Triads

Compare to these different keys:

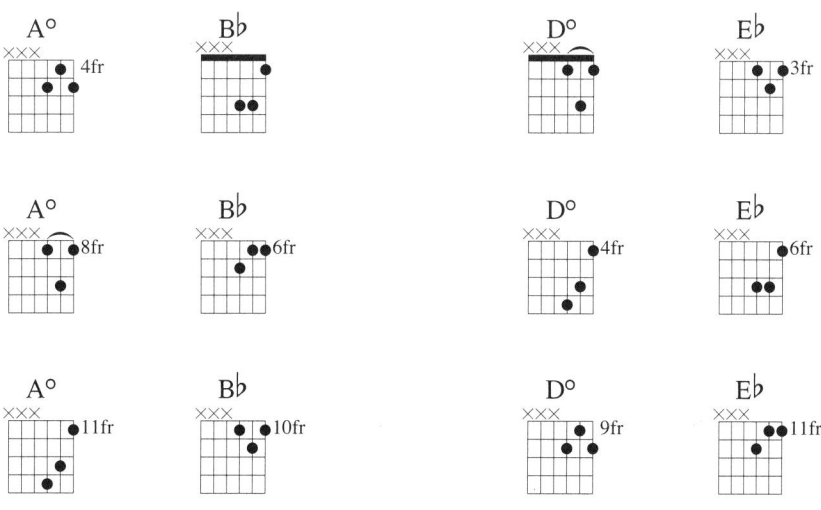

FIG. 3.5. A° to B♭   **FIG. 3.6.** D° to E♭

Now move these forms around to create other diminished triads and notice which notes fall on the highest E string. If you are quick at the theory of chord construction, you will have an easy time of moving these chord forms around the neck to land on other diminished triads.

Here are some examples:

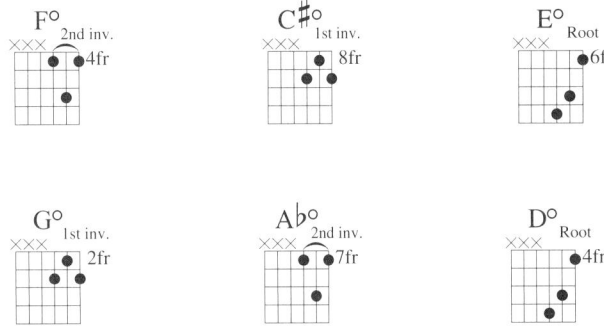

FIG. 3.7. Random Diminished Triads

Before looking at the answers, write the chord tone below the note on the first string on each chord diagram.

Answers here:

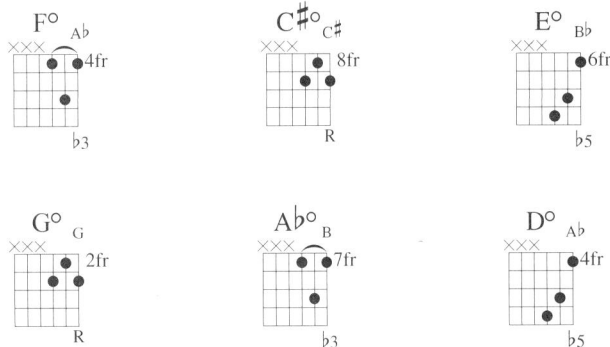

FIG. 3.8. First String Chord Tone I.D.

CHAPTER 4

Augmented Triads

Augmented triads contain two major third intervals, with an augmented fifth from the root to the fifth of the chord. The formula for an augmented triad is R 3 ♯5. Reference an E♭ major scale to identify an E♭+ triad as such. B♭ is the fifth note of an E♭ major scale, B natural, therefore, is the sharp five, or augmented fifth.

Augmented triads do not occur naturally in a major scale. However, you will find them in melodic minor scales, harmonic minor scales, and harmonic major scales.

Here is a quick look at the way the triads stack up naturally in each of those scales:

FIG. 4.1. Melodic Minor Triads, Harmonic Minor Triads, Harmonic Major Triads

The III chord in both melodic minor and harmonic minor scales is an augmented triad. The VI chord in a harmonic major scale is an augmented triad.

Augmented triads have an unstable sound, often used to alter or spice up a V chord resolving to its I chord, as in G+ to C.

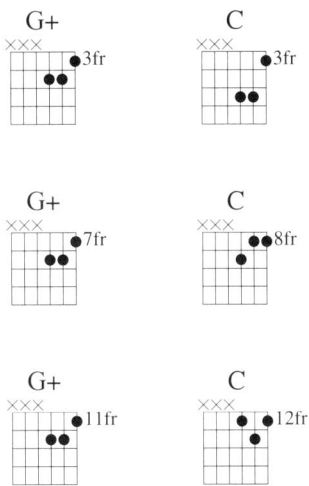

FIG. 4.2. G+ to C All Inversions on the First Three Strings

A *whole tone* scale is full of augmented triads.

FIG. 4.3. Whole Tone Scale

Making use of enharmonic spelling, you can identify every triad built on each scale degree of the whole tone scale as augmented.

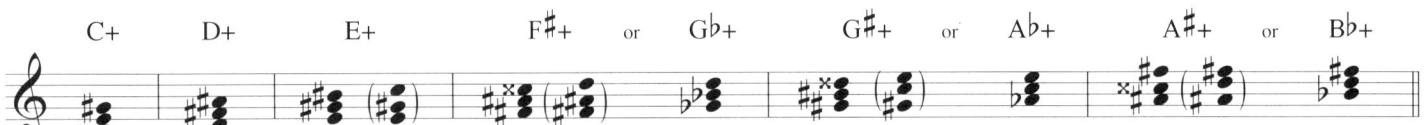

FIG. 4.4. Triads in a Whole Tone Scale

No wonder whole tone scales sound so good played over augmented chords!

CHAPTER 5

The Triads, Organized

Now that you have committed each triad type to memory, both in theory and in chord forms on the fretboard, here is a view to recap and organize them all on the first three strings:

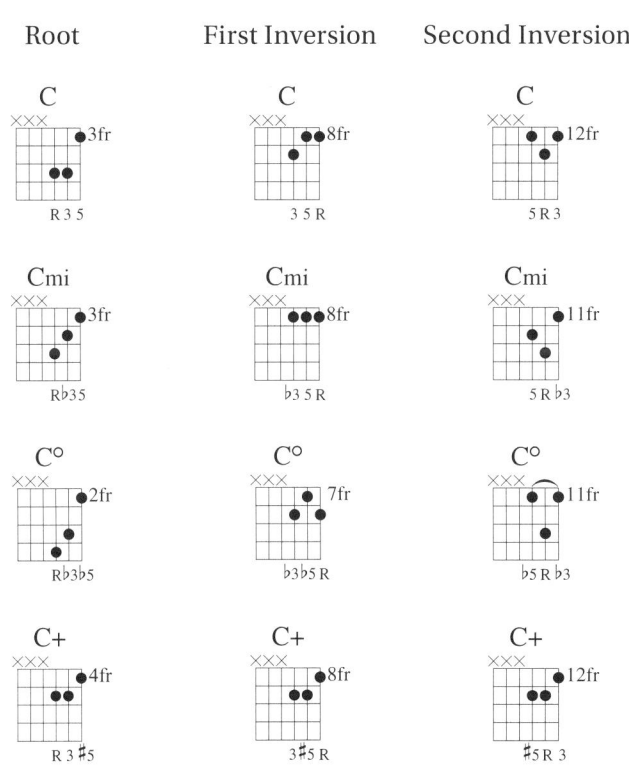

FIG. 5.1. Triad List

PART II
Larger Chords and Triads

CHAPTER 6

Major 7 Chords and Their Matched Minor Triads

A major 7 chord formula is R 3 5 7. Simply add the seventh note of the major scale to a major triad. CMaj7 = C E G B.

FIG. 6.1. CMaj7

In addition to CMaj7 containing a C major triad in its three lowest notes, it also contains an E minor triad in its three highest notes.

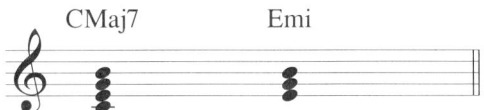

FIG. 6.2. CMaj7 and Emi

Suppose you are playing from a lead sheet with other musicians, and you see the chord CMaj7. You could play it in any of the common voicings for a major 7 chord that you might know.

FIG. 6.3. CMaj7 Voicings

Maybe there's a bass player, or a pianist, or another guitar player supplying the root of the chord. Or maybe you are playing a chord melody solo and you have established the sound of the CMaj7, but you'd like to be able to move it to another position on the fretboard without needing to play the root. Seeing that the Emi triad sits right on top of that CMaj7 chord means that you can play an Emi triad in any inversion or position and consider it a CMaj7 chord.

Here again are the three positions for an Emi triad on the first three strings, this time paired with C in the bass clef:

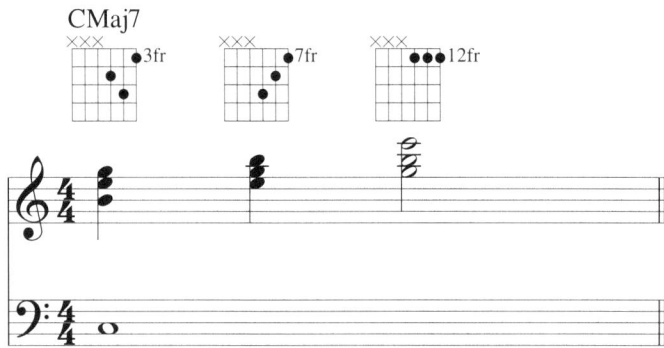

FIG. 6.4. CMaj7 Chords Played as Emi Triads

Now do the exercise of naming the notes again, as you did for the triads in part I. This time, however, indicate the chord tones as they relate to CMaj7 instead of Emi.

Answers are here:

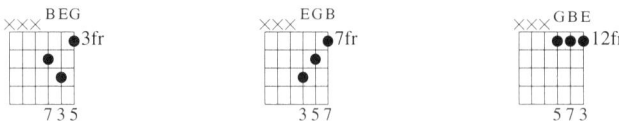

FIG. 6.5. Chord Tones for CMaj7

Notice that there is no root of the major 7 chord in these voicings, only the 3, 5, and 7. Since only the first three strings are being used here, something had to give; the root is easily replaced by the 7 in these voicings. You could think of these forms as beginning with C major triads, identifying the root, and then lowering the root by one-half step.

Here are the three inversions of a C triad followed by their corresponding major 7 voicing:

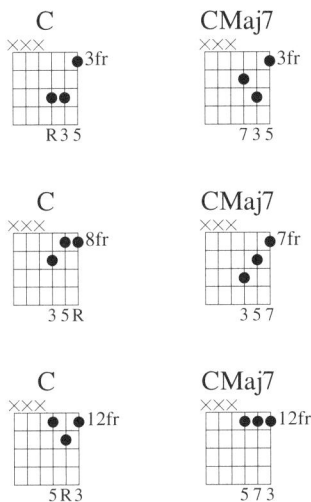

FIG. 6.6. C Triads with Related Major 7 Chords

You're left with the three Emi triads! You'll quickly be able to eliminate the step between the C triad and the CMaj7 and just think of the Emi form in a new way.

Paying careful attention to the note and the chord tone that is on the first string will now provide you with the shortcuts you'll need to move these chord forms around the neck to play your nearest CMaj7. Even though the fingerings are the same as what has been used for Emi, the context has changed, and the notes to follow on the E string will be your new reference as you transpose major 7 chords all over the neck. The first chord form, formerly thought of as Emi second inversion, will now be CMaj7 with G (5) on top. Emi from the root becomes CMaj7 with the Maj7 (B) on top. And Emi first inversion becomes CMaj7 with the 3 (E) on top.

Using a I to IV progression, which are both major 7 chords in a given major key, play around the cycle of fourths to practice finding the associated minor triad fingerings in each key and for each major 7 chord.

Here is the progression, first shown by only the chord name:

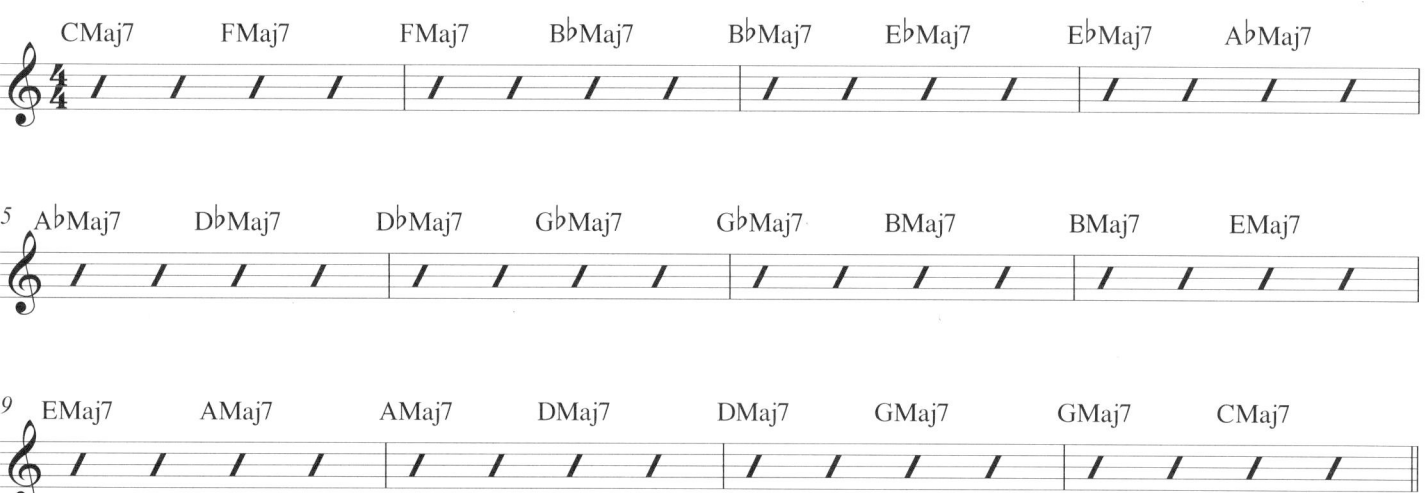

FIG. 6.7. Cycle of Fourths Major 7 Chords

You might first play this progression in whatever way you may know these chord forms. Go ahead and make a backing track for yourself of these major 7 chords. Give yourself time to get through all twelve keys. As you play the track back, play along live to it by using the corresponding minor triads for each major 7 chord. If you use the shortcut, you'll find that having learned the three different minor triad chord forms is the important first step; finding their place on the fretboard as major 7 chords for any key is the essential application for this method. If you're quick at theory and chord spelling, you'll be able to think ahead for each chord in the progression to land on the nearest chord tone of the next chord.

One way through this is shown in figure 6.8. Let your ears help you to make the match between the three-string chord and the root in the bass part.

CHAPTER 6. Major 7 Chords and Their Matched Minor Triads (Miller)

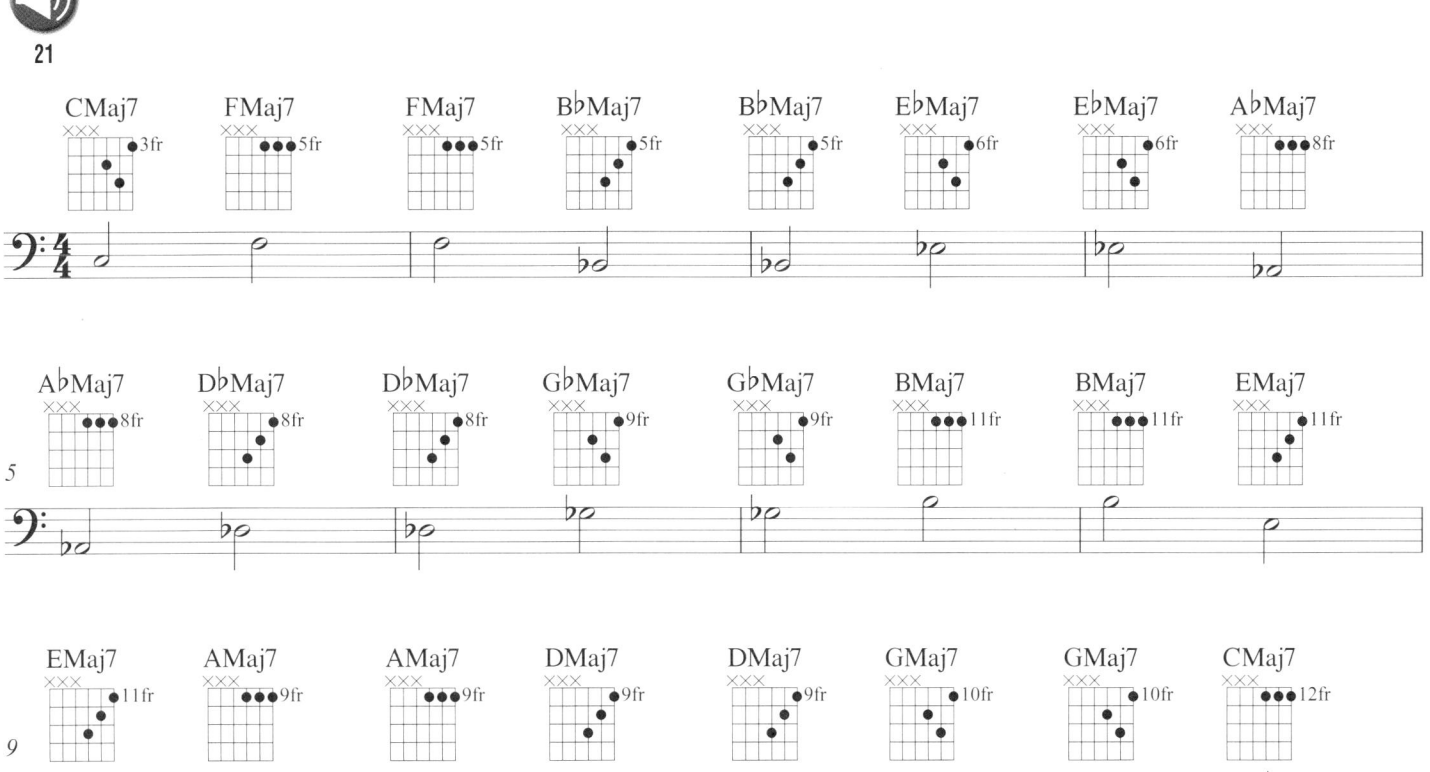

FIG. 6.8. Voice-Led Cycle 4 Major 7 Chords

If you start on the Emi second inversion, giving you a G (the 5) of the CMaj7 chord on top, the rest of your choices will be made by considering whatever chords are the closest to that first voicing. Since there is no G in FMaj7, the nearest chord tone to the next chord is A. Using the Ami with the root on the first string, or first inversion, will work well. Leaving the A on top gives you the 7 of the B♭Maj7; the rest of the Dmi triad can be formed under that note as a root position Dmi. After a while, you won't even think of that chord form as Dmi, but rather you'll see it as B♭Maj7 when you need it.

If we continue by moving higher up the neck, we'll find that the B♭ on the sixth fret of the E string is a good next step to turn a G minor second inversion triad into an E♭Maj7.

Keep going in an ascending direction, and you'll find that a C minor triad can be used for the A♭Maj7 chord. By now, you might see that the name of each of these minor triads that corresponds to the major 7 chords being played all begin on the third of the major 7 chord. If you are quick to find those triads in voice-led fashion and in time through the cycle, then that can be a useful shortcut for you. If following the high note works well for you, then you will see that connection as you go through the repetition of finding and playing these chord forms and listening to their match with the bass notes and low-voiced seventh chords.

If, instead, you start the whole progression at the 7th fret position with B as the high note of the CMaj7, the closest FMaj7 will be at the 8th fret, the nearest BbMaj7 will be at the 10th fret, EbMaj7 also at the 10th fret. At some point in that high fret neighborhood, you might want to head back toward the low frets, especially if you don't have a cutaway on your guitar. Figure 6.9 shows a way to descend once you reach DbMaj7 at the 13th fret. It's a judgment call, but if you're running out of frets, there's always a way back. GbMaj7 could have been played at the 13th, 14th, and 15th frets as a Bbmi triad in root position, but instead, here it is back at the 9th, 10th, and 11th frets.

Shortcut: look for the 5 of the GbMaj7 chord, which is Db on the first string. It's still a Bbmi triad, this time with the b3 on top, but with practice and the mental exercise that comes from thinking through the progression as major 7 chords, you'll be able to eliminate the minor triad as part of the thought process.

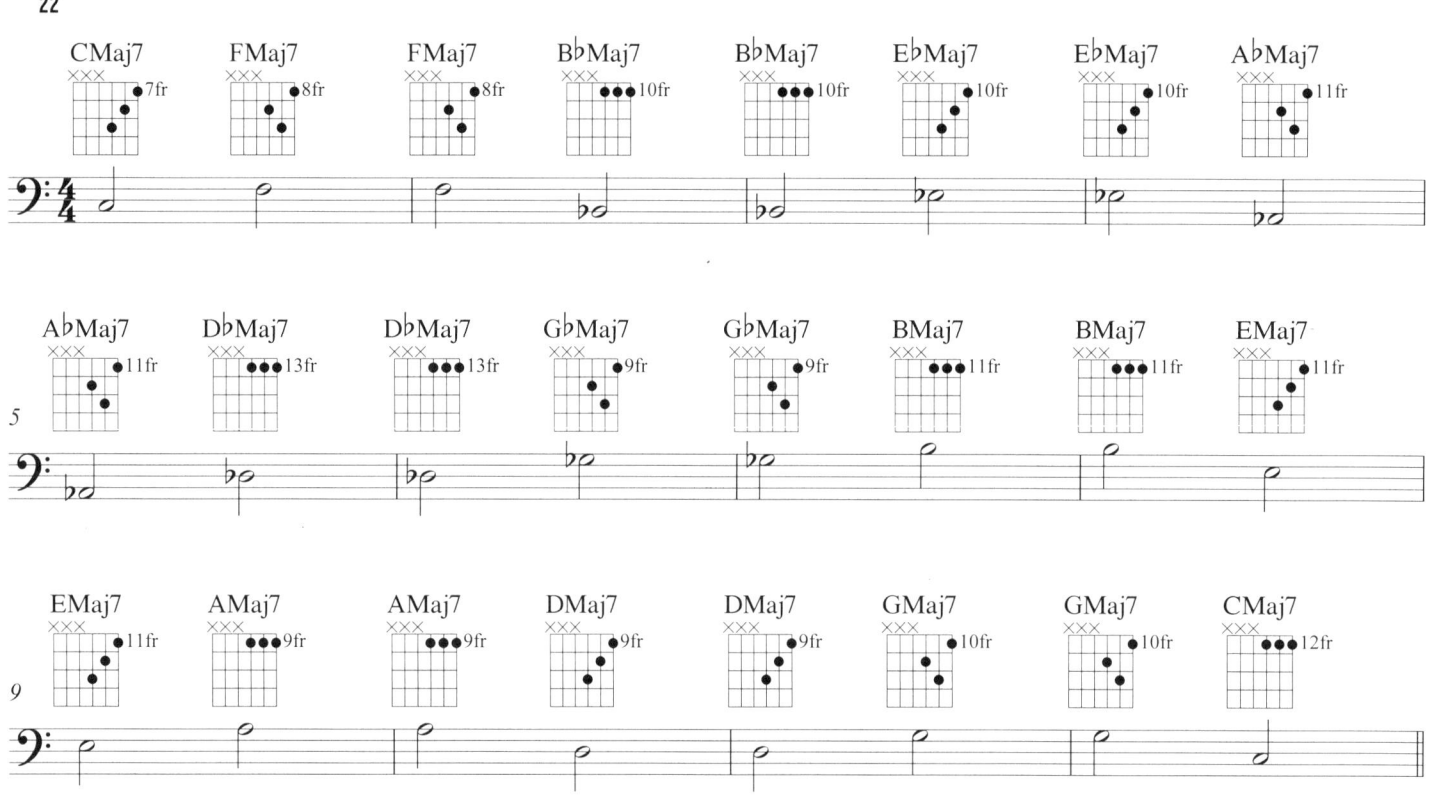

FIG. 6.9. Cycle 4 Major 7 Chords Second Option

Finally, try starting the CMaj7 chord at the 12th fret and then work your way down the fretboard. You might see this as one step forward, two steps back, since you can ascend to the FMaj7, keeping the high E as a common tone, and then jump back to BbMaj7 at the 10th fret with EbMaj7 also at the 10th fret, continuing the same pattern all the way down the neck.

CHAPTER 6. Major 7 Chords and Their Matched Minor Triads

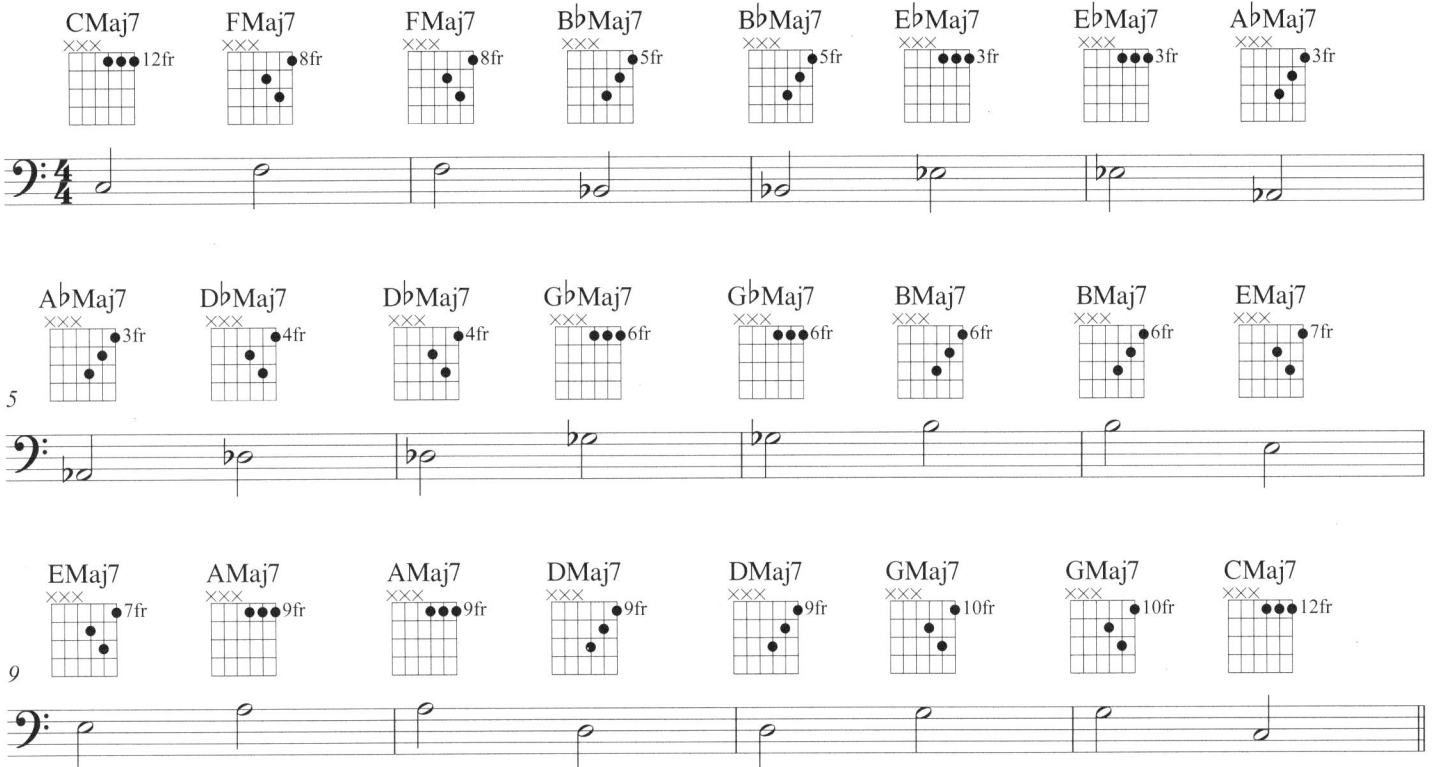

FIG. 6.10. Cycle 4 Major 7 Chords Third Option

Now practice randomizing some major 7 chords all over the first three strings. Move in either direction, jump to any interval in the root motion, listen to the chord tone that falls on the top note, and name each chord as you land on it. Use the major 7 name rather than the triad name. Record yourself doing this, and then play back the root to bring the chord into focus.

Here's my version:

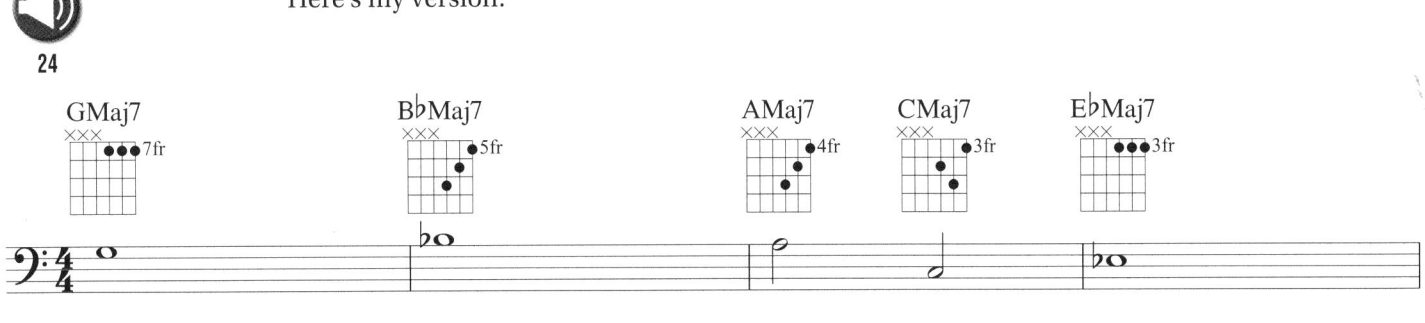

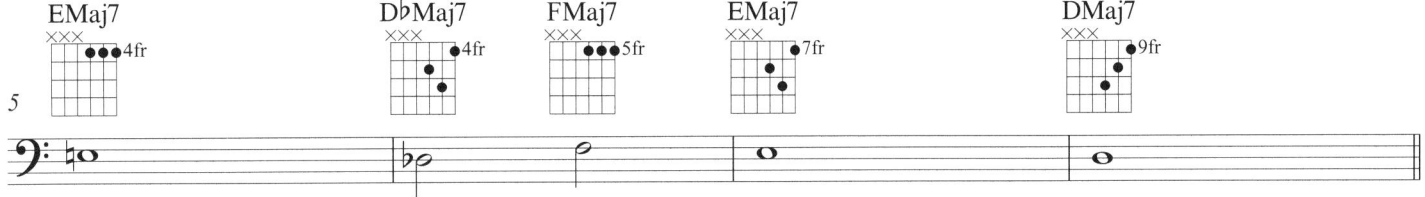

FIG. 6.11. Random Major 7 Chord Progression

CHAPTER 7

Minor 7 Chords and Their Matched Major Triads

The formula for a minor 7 chord is R ♭3 5 ♭7 from its corresponding major scale. Cmi7= C E♭ G B♭. In addition to the Cmi triad in the lowest notes of this chord, there is an E♭ major triad sitting on top.

FIG. 7.1. Cmi7, E♭

Listen to a C bass note as you play all three inversion of the E♭ triad on the first three strings. The new context will have your ears alerting you to a minor 7 chord quality.

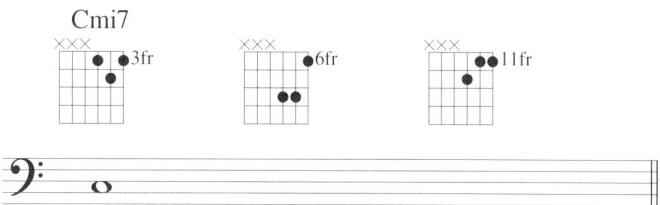

FIG. 7.2. Cmi7: E♭ with C in Bass

You have done the work to now know that the first E♭ triad shown (second inversion) has a G, or 3 on top. The root position E♭ has the B♭ or 5 on top, and the first inversion has the E♭ or root on top. Now, as with the major 7 chords, begin to shift your thinking so that the new context is as follows: Cmi7 with G on top is the 5, Cmi7 with B♭ on top is ♭7, and Cmi7 with E♭ on top is ♭3.

CHAPTER 7. Minor 7 Chords and Their Matched Major Triads (Miller)

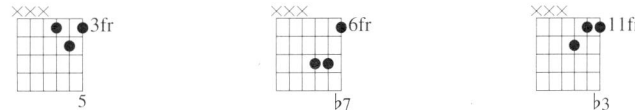

FIG. 7.3. Cmi7 with Chord Tones on First String

Here is a minor blues-based progression using all minor 7 chords:

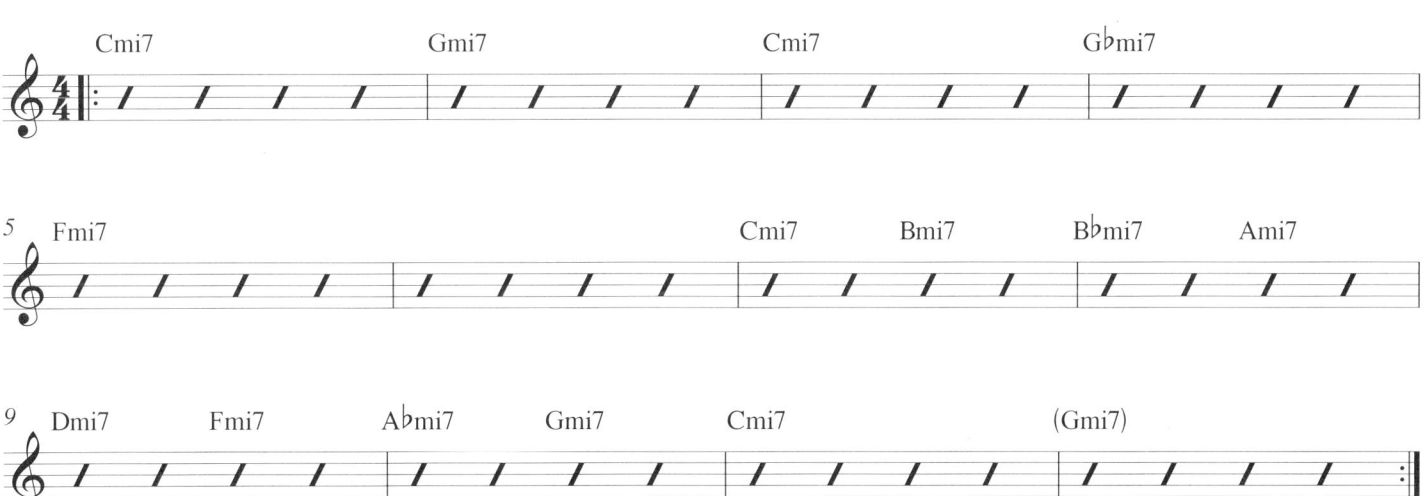

FIG. 7.4. Minor Blues-Based Progression

Play this progression three times using different major triad options each time. Make it your goal to voice lead the progression; minimize your movements from one chord to the next, and find the most efficient changes. When you're ready to compare notes, three answers are shown in figure 7.5.

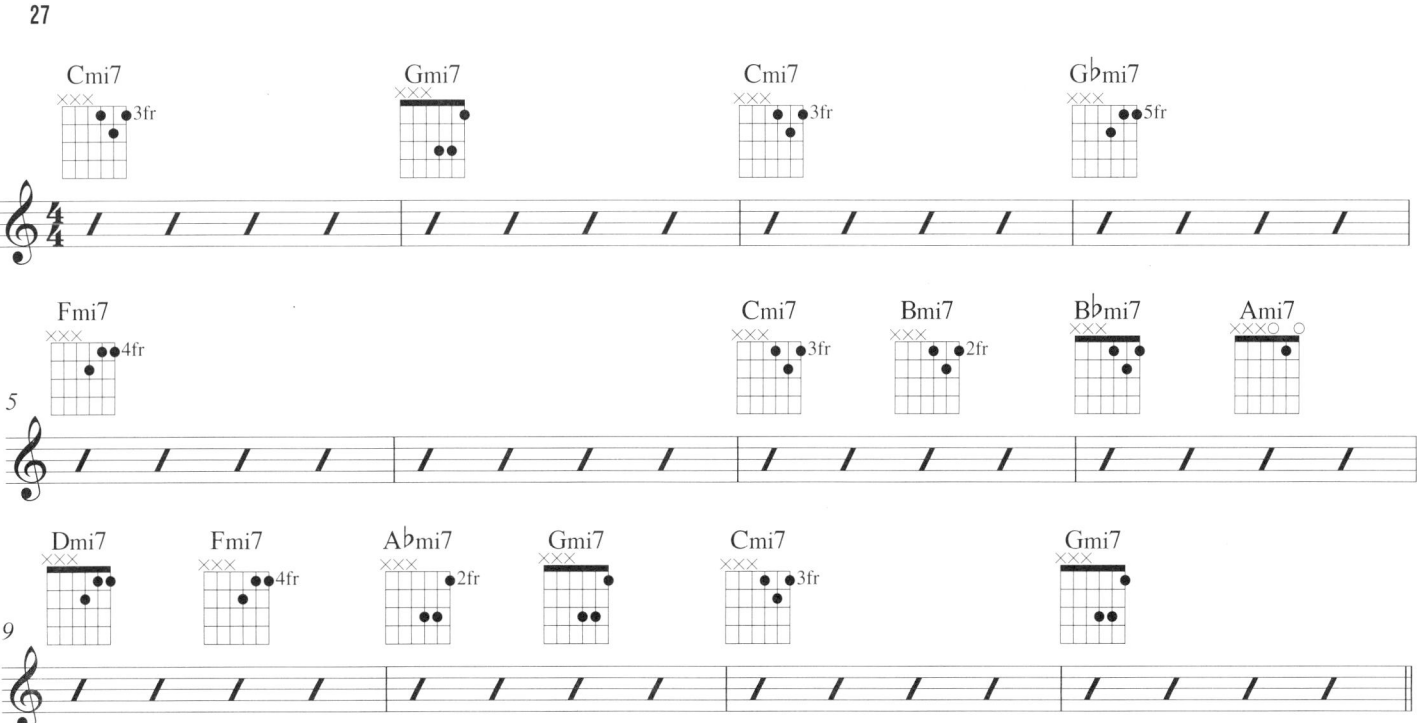

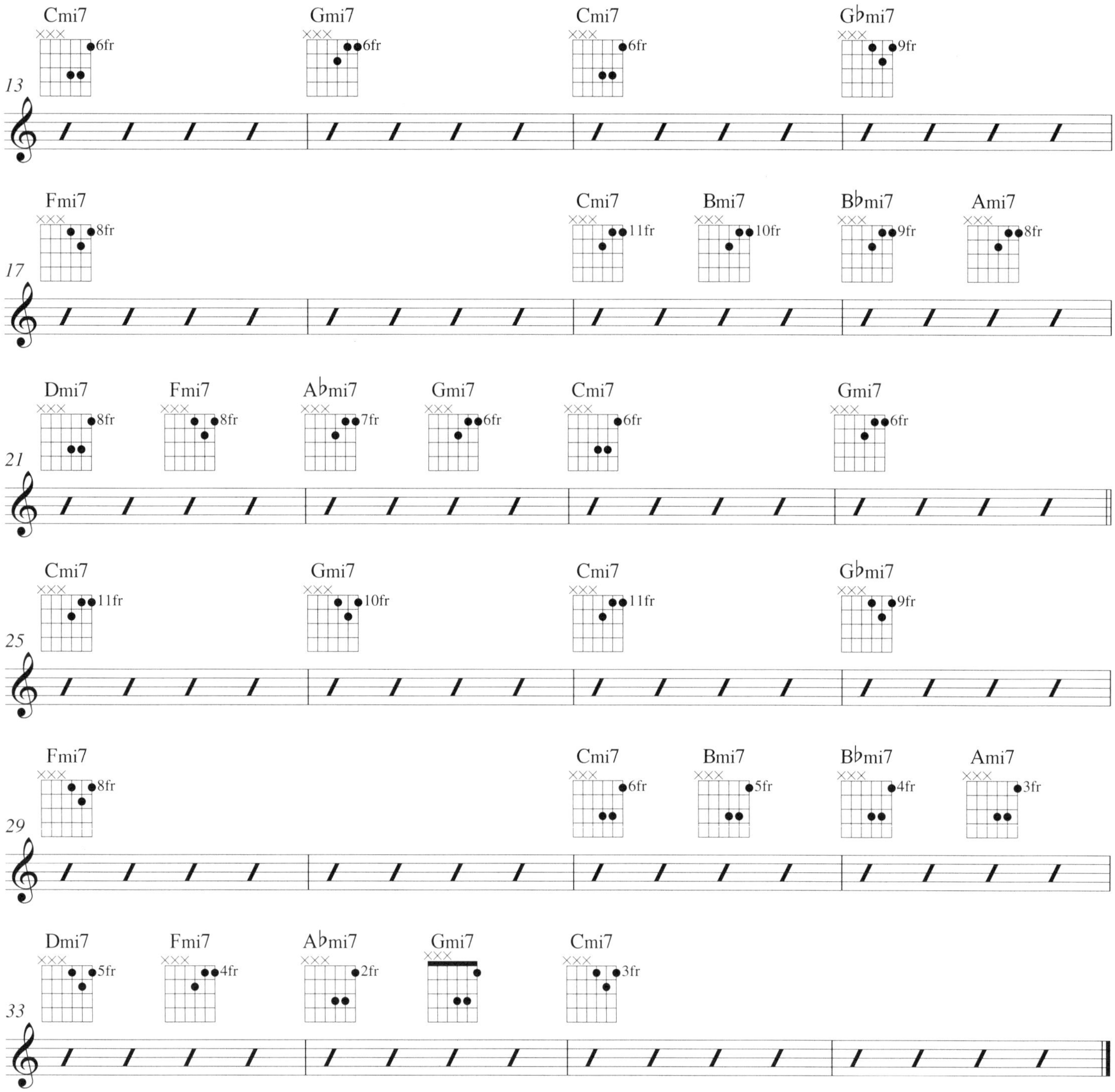

FIG. 7.5. Three Times Through Minor Progression

As you work this out, you will be aware of which major triads fit with the minor 7 chords. As you practice, make it a habit to think in the context of minor 7 chords on three strings rather than major triads. Go back to the diagrams and name the chord tones on the high E string as they relate to the minor 7 chords.

Answers below:

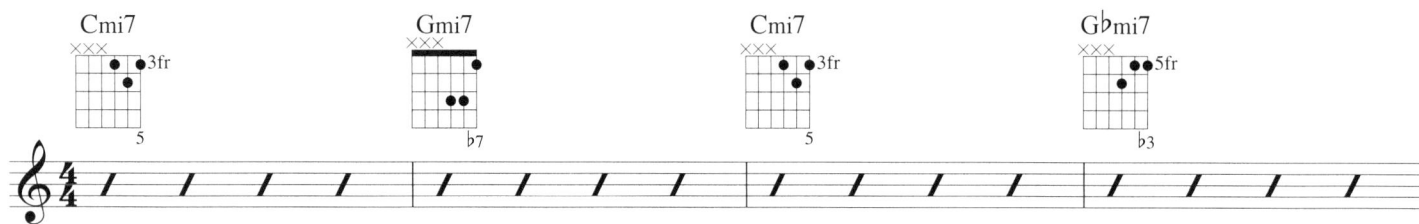

CHAPTER 7. Minor 7 Chords and Their Matched Major Triads (Miller)

FIG. 7.6. Chord Tones on E String

CHAPTER 8

Dominant 7 Chords Matched with Diminished Triads

The formula for a dominant 7 chord is R 3 5 ♭7 from the major scale sharing the name with the root of the chord. C7 = C E G B♭.

FIG. 8.1. C7

The three lowest notes are, of course, a C major triad. Sitting on top of that in the three highest notes is an E° triad, or E G B♭.

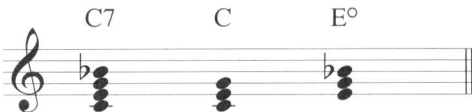

FIG. 8.2. C7: C and E°

Refer to the diminished triads in chapter 3 to review the three inversions on the first three strings.

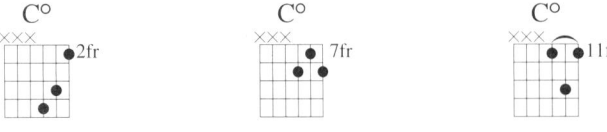

FIG. 8.3. C° Root, First Inversion, Second Inversion

CHAPTER 8. Dominant 7 Chords Matched with Diminished Triads (Miller)

Now transpose those diminished triads to another root by first noticing what chord tone falls on the high E string.

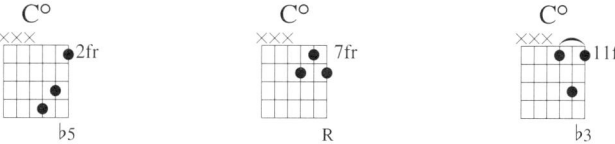

FIG. 8.4. C° Chord Tones on First String

Let's transpose it to E°. Getting quick at the theory, you'll then see that the ♭5 of E is B♭, the root is E, and the ♭3 is G. Adjust the positions of the C° triad inversions to match those chord tones on the first string to land on E°.

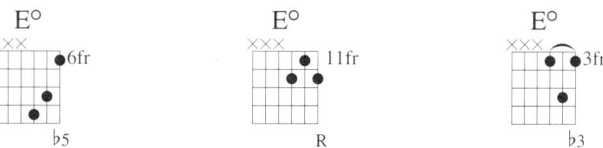

FIG. 8.5. E° with B♭, E, and G on the High String

Once you've done that, you can use those triad forms to play on a C7. Shift your thinking to identify the chord tones to relate to C7 instead of E°. Now, the B♭ on the first string will be the ♭7, the E on the first string will be the 3, and the G on the first string will be the 5 of the chord. Memorizing those voicings in this new way gives you the luxury of using chord forms that your fingers have already learned. Your musical brain and mind's ear will guide you in a new direction when you're navigating your way around dominant 7 chords.

Here's a three-chord blues to put these diminished triad forms—now to be considered dominant 7 chords—to use in this common format.

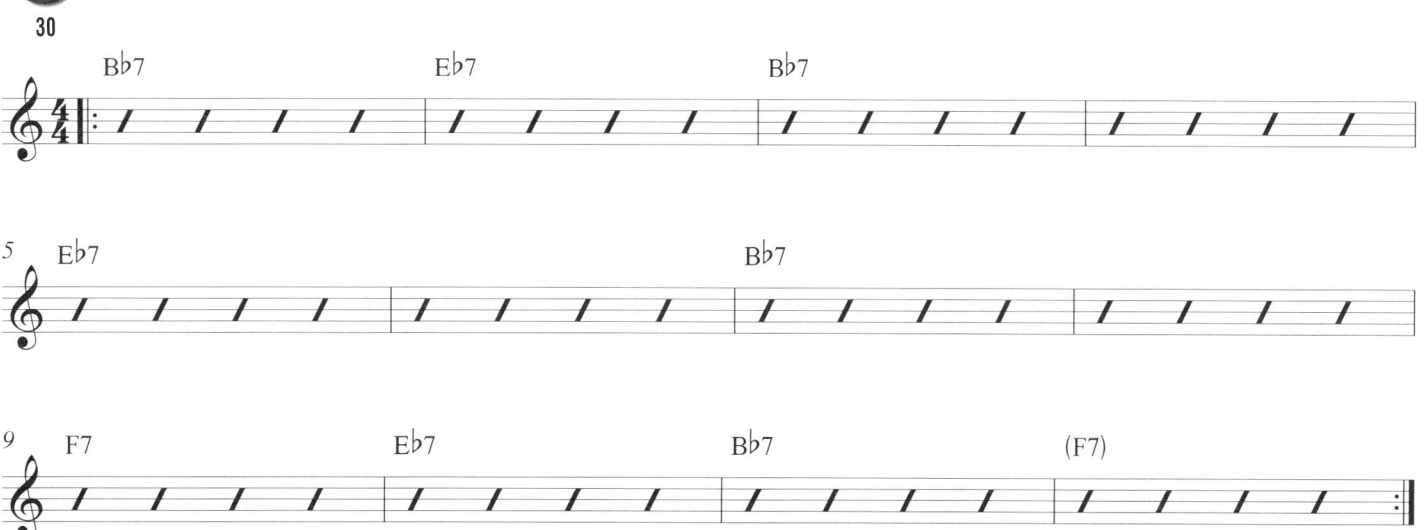

FIG. 8.6. 12-Bar Blues in B♭

I recommend making your own backing tracks (mine is provided here, in track 30) so that you can practice comping the chords however you'd like. Then play the small, three-string forms live along with the track.

Next, try it in F.

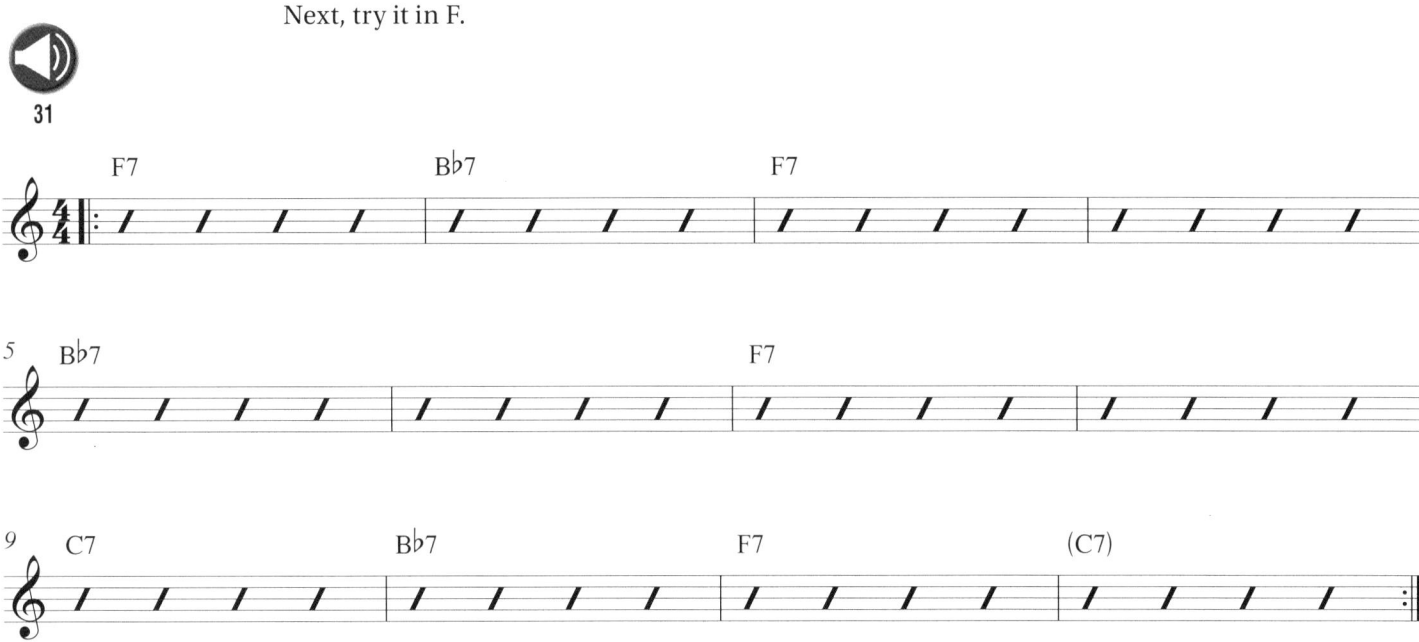

FIG. 8.7. 12-Bar Blues in F

You can go through each of these blues progressions three times and play them a different way each time, since you know three different inversions of the associated diminished triad forms.

When you're ready to compare your three-string progression ideas to some of mine, look at these three ways through the blues in B♭:

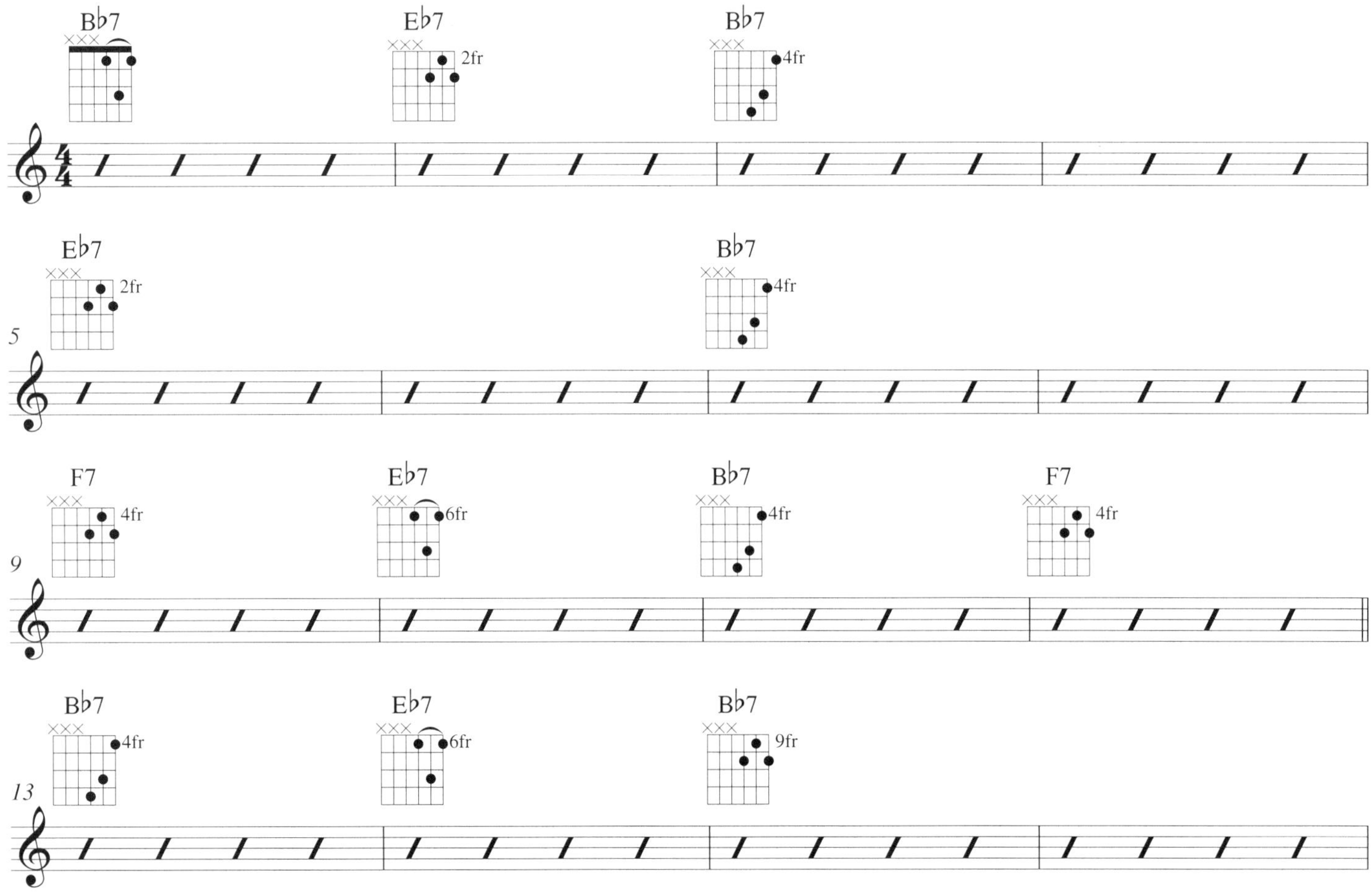

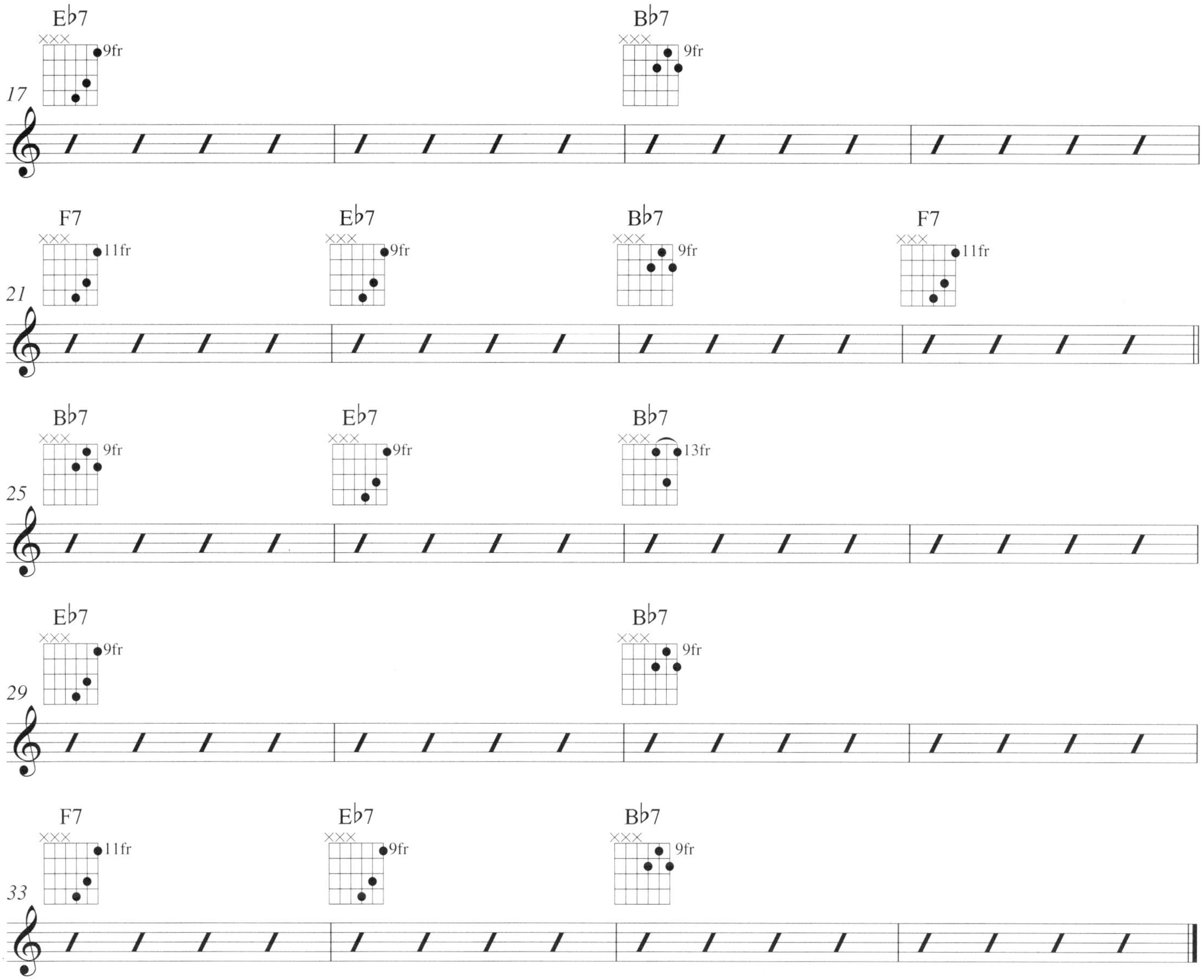

CHAPTER 8. Dominant 7 Chords Matched with Diminished Triads (Miller)

FIG. 8.8. Three Choruses of Blues in B♭

And now three times through blues in F:

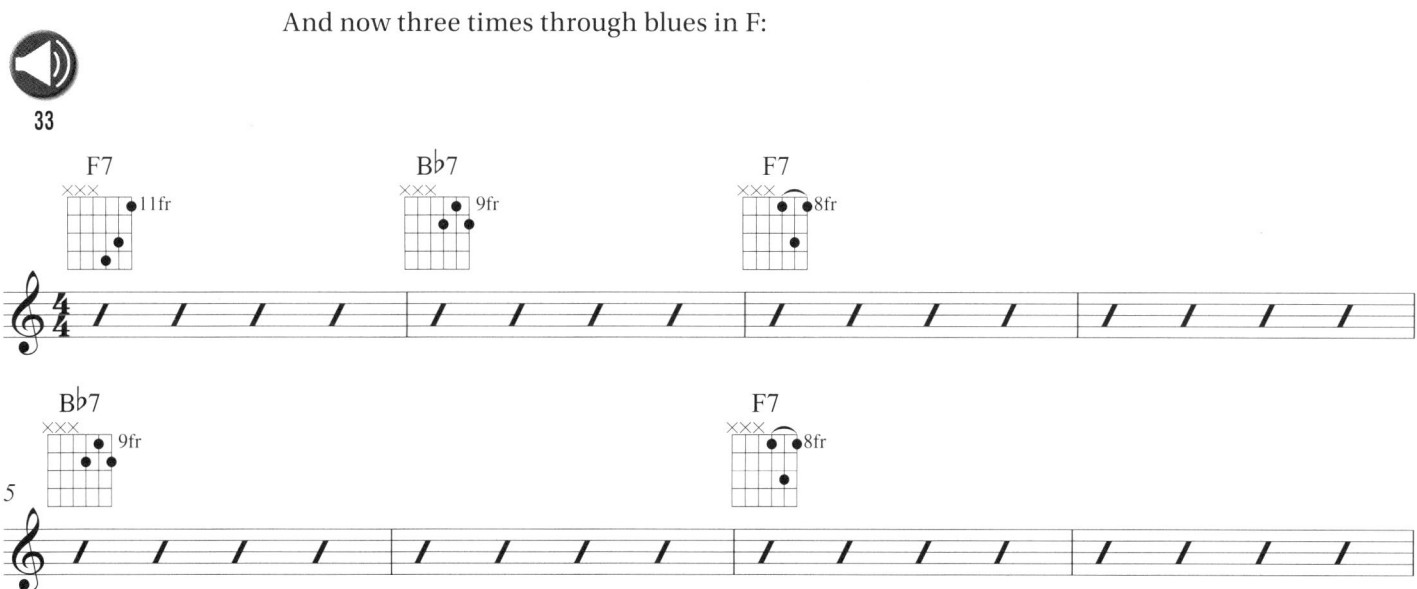

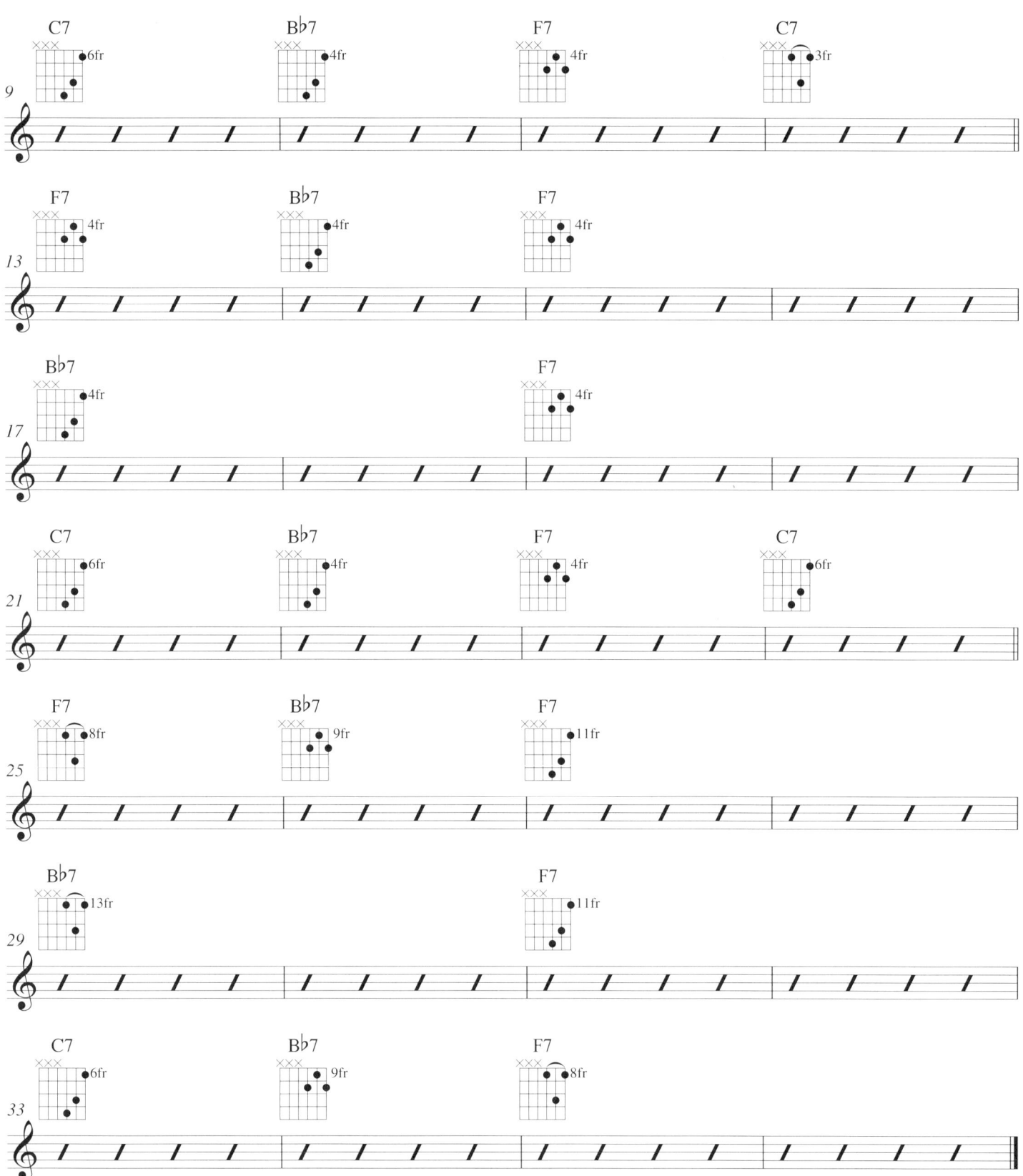

FIG. 8.9. Three Choruses of Blues in F

CHAPTER 9

Minor 7♭5 Chords

The formula for minor 7♭5 chords is R ♭3 ♭5 ♭7. Their name is a wonderfully explicit description of what they are: a minor 7 chord with a flat 5. They are also sometimes called half-diminished chords, since they contain a diminished triad in the lowest three notes. From the root to the ♭7 is the same interval as in a minor 7 chord and a dominant 7 chord. A Cmi7♭5 contains the notes C E♭ G♭ B♭.

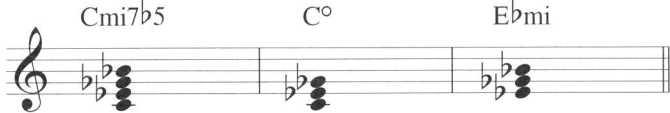

FIG. 9.1. Cmi7♭5, C°, and E♭mi

The top three notes of this chord are E♭, G♭, and B♭, which is an E♭ minor triad. Any minor 7♭5 chord will contain the minor triad which is built on the ♭3 of the chord.

Try it out:

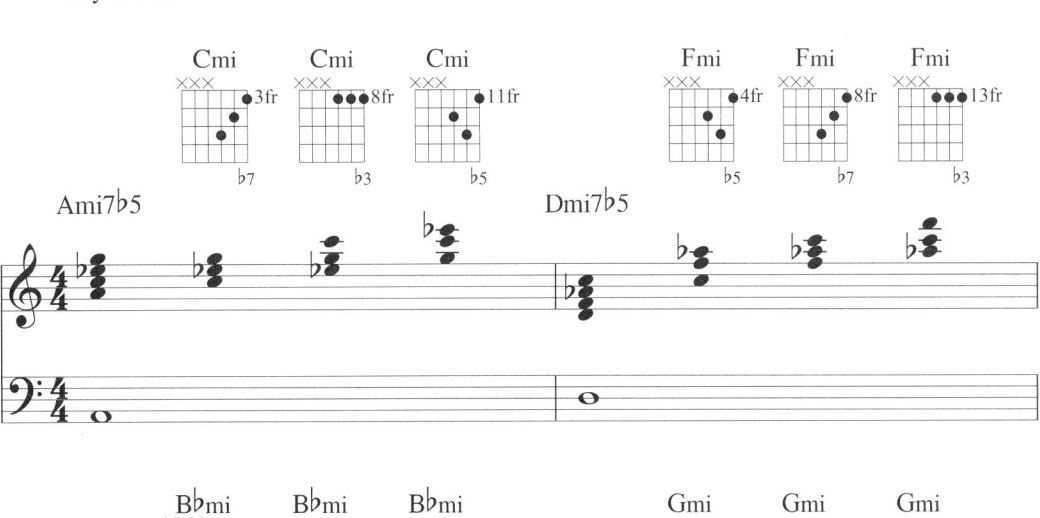

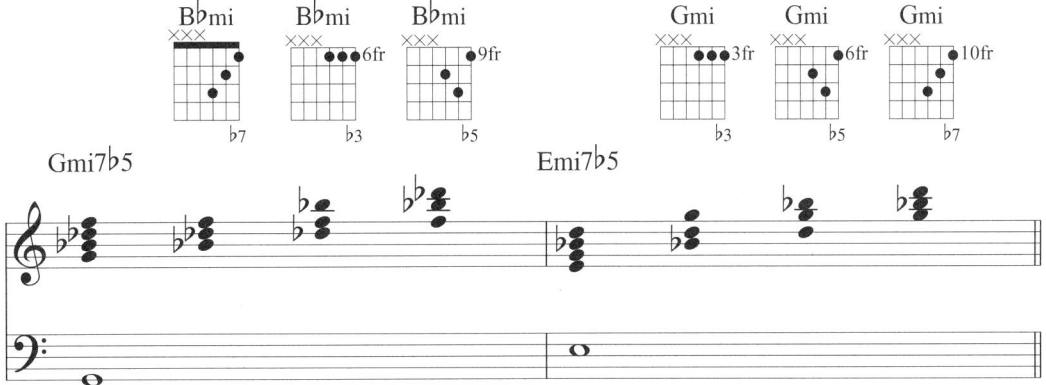

FIG. 9.2. Minor 7♭5 Chords with Minor Triads

Use any inversion of a minor triad to play a minor 7b5 chord. From now on, think of those triad shapes as the chord tones relate to the minor 7b5 chord. Thinking this way, Ami7b5 can be played with the b7, b3, or b5 as the high note. What you previously thought of as Cmi triads with the 5 (G), root (C), or b3 (Eb) on top, can now be thought of as Ami7b5 chords with the b7 (G), b3 (C), or b5 (Eb) on top.

Here is a progression with some typical uses of the minor 7b5 chords in combination with other seventh chords:

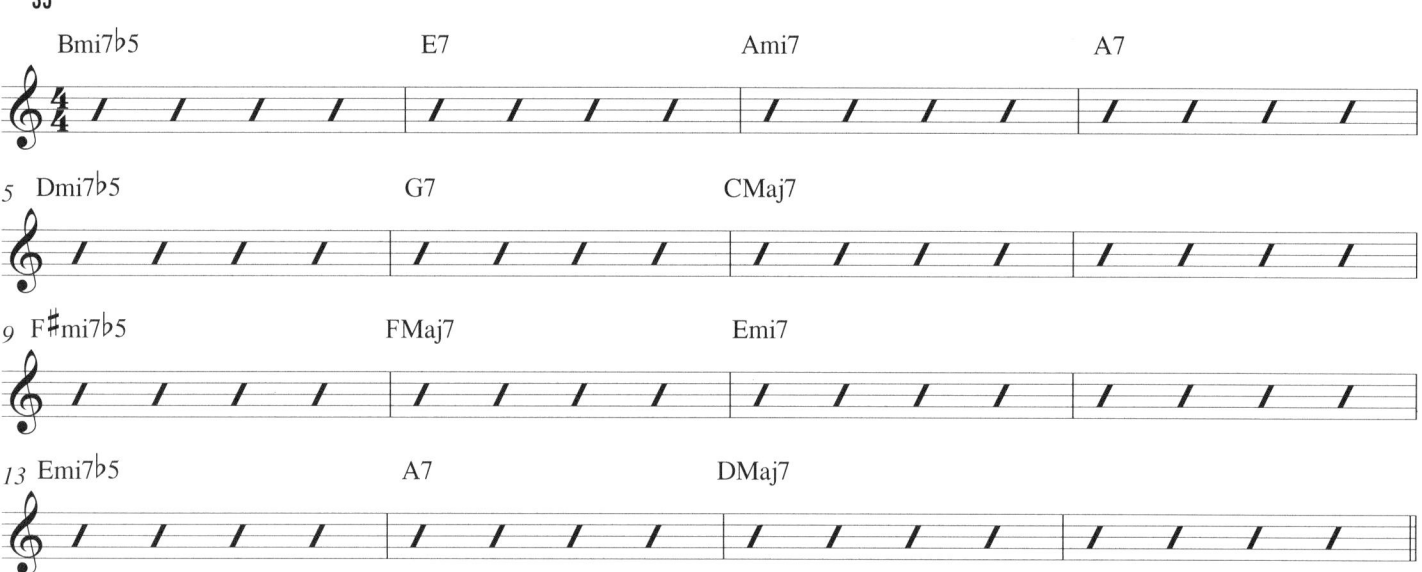

FIG. 9.3. Minor 7b5 Chords with Other Seventh Chords

CHAPTER 9. Minor 7♭5 Chords

Practice playing this progression three times, using different three-string chord forms each time around. Your goal should be to change to the closest possible choice of chord form as you move from one chord to the next. Here are three possibilities to examine and play once you've tried out your own.

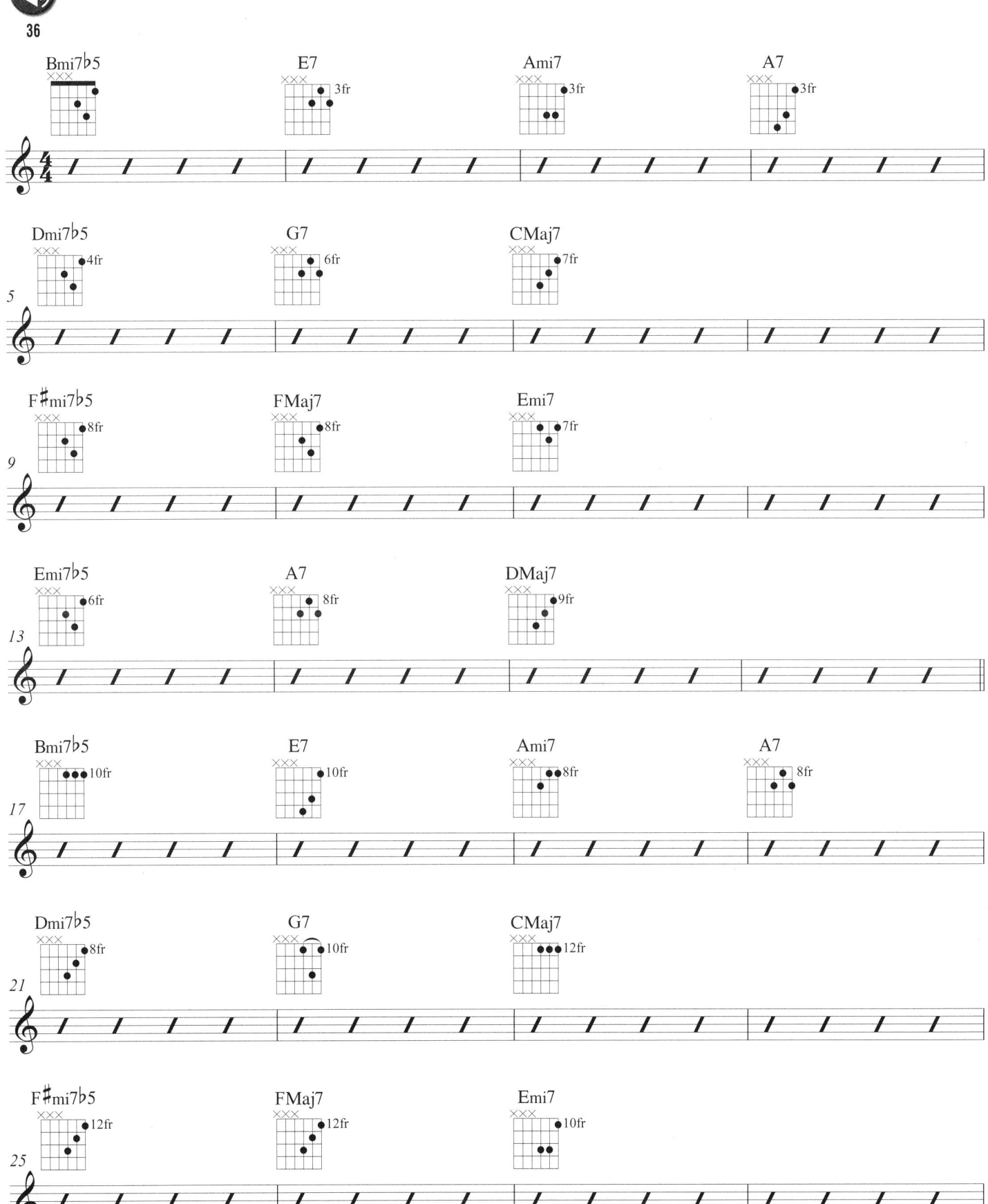

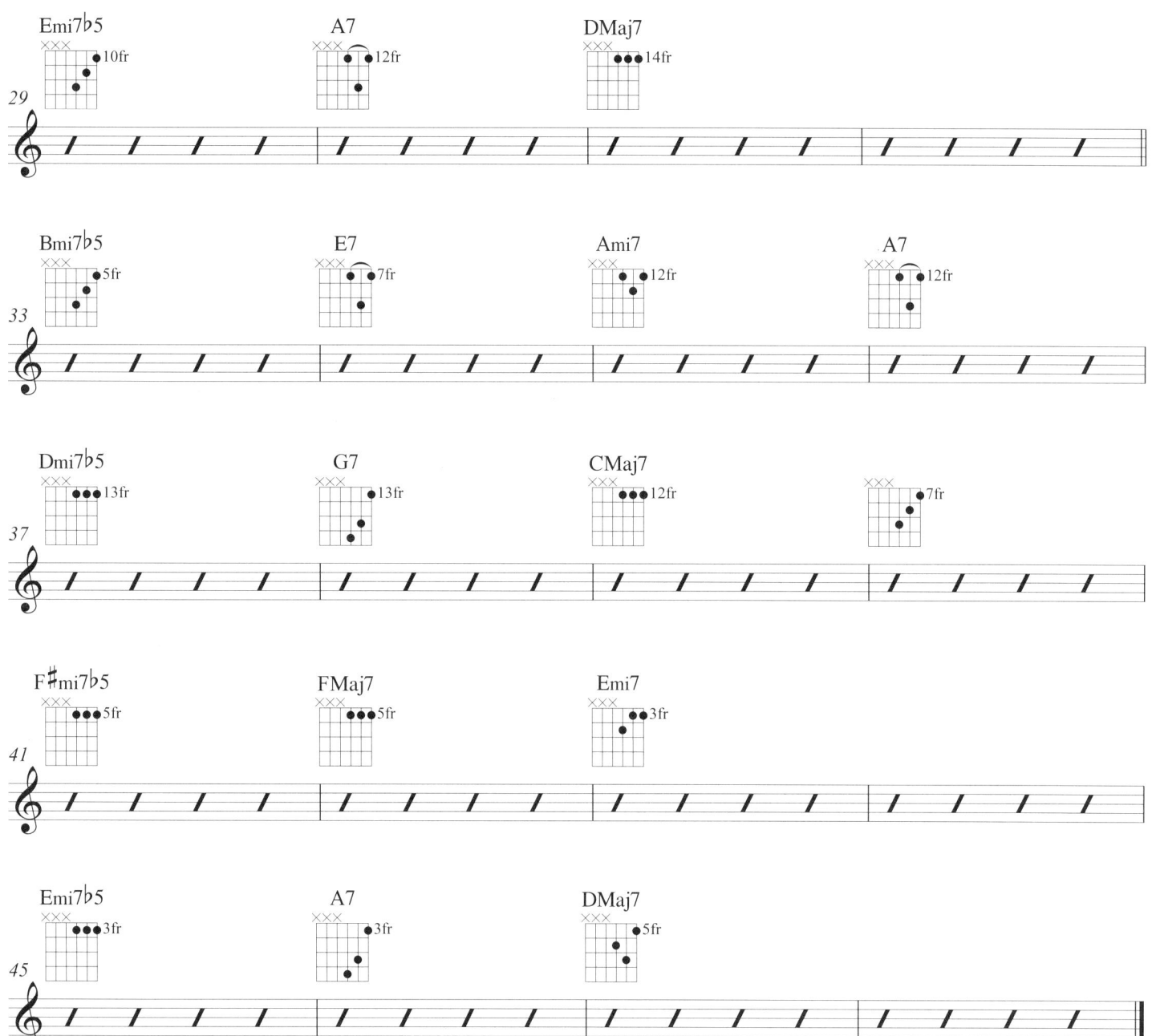

FIG. 9.4. Three Ways to Play Mixed Seventh Chords

CHAPTER 10

Diminished 7 Chords

Diminished 7 chords are an interesting set of four notes: 1 ♭3 ♭5 ♭♭7. There is an interval of a minor third between each note, even counting the interval between the ♭♭7 and the octave root. C°7 contains the notes C E♭ G♭ and B♭♭, or A. The ♭♭7 is the same note name as 6, and we'll use that as a short cut to name the note.

FIG. 10.1. C°7

Play any diminished 7 chord on the guitar, move it three frets in either direction, and you'll be playing an inversion of the same chord you started on.

FIG. 10.2. E♭°7 Inversions

This particular seventh chord type will be treated differently from the other seventh chords in that you will stick to diminished triads as a reference rather than a triad with a different quality from the seventh chord. Another difference to notice is that the triad you use can either represent the three lowest notes of the seventh chord, or the three highest. So, a C°7 contains a C° triad and also an E♭° triad. While you're at it, you can go ahead and use G♭° and A° triads, too!

FIG. 10.3. C°7 Chord and Its Triads

Every diminished 7 chord can be named by any of its chord tones, since they are all inversions of the same chord. This means that there are only three different diminished 7 chords: C°7, C#°7, and D°7, going chromatically.

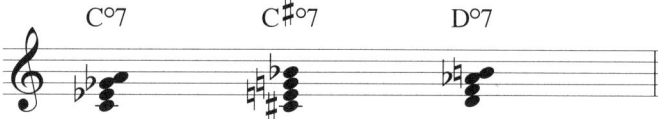

FIG. 10.4. C°7, C#°7, and D°7

As long as you stay within the same chord "family," you can use four different diminished triads to play over a diminished 7 chord. Here are the three different diminished 7 chords and their corresponding four choices of triad matches:

FIG. 10.5. Diminished 7 Chords and Their Triad Matches

CHAPTER 10. Diminished 7 Chords (Miller)

Some choices of fingerings for these seventh chords and their corresponding triads:

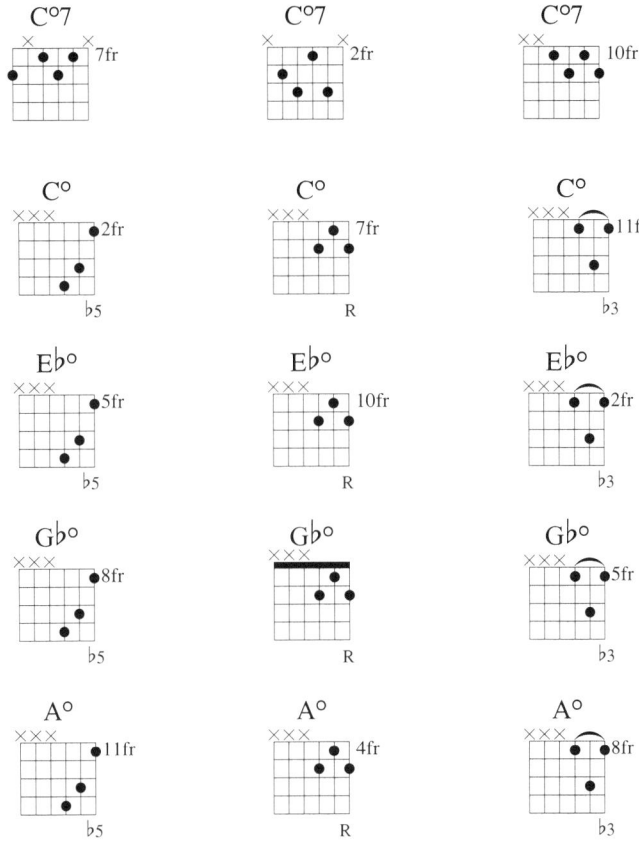

FIG. 10.6. Diminished 7 Chords Voicings and Their Related Triads

Here's a progression using some typical diminished seven chord placements in the harmony:

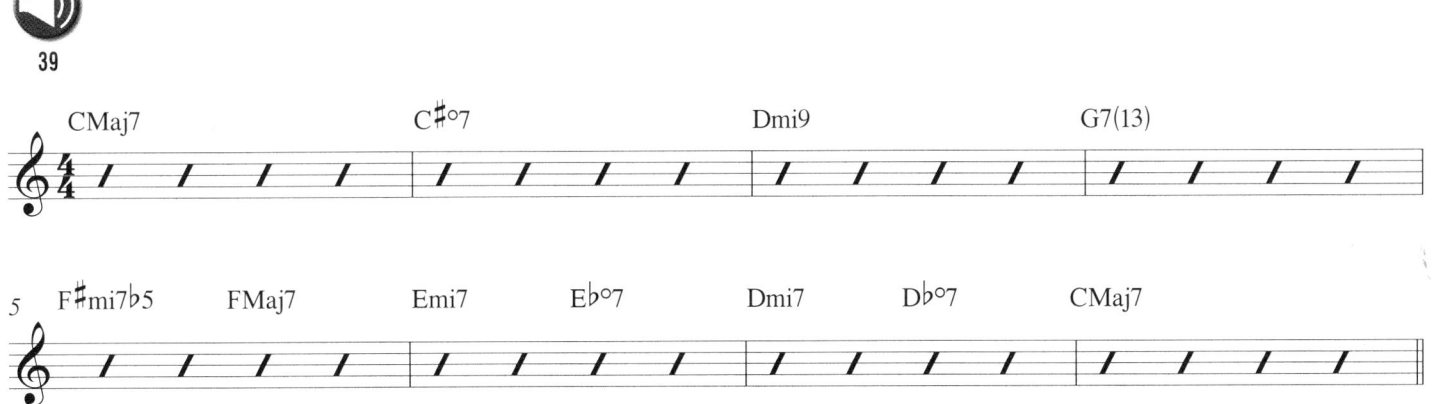

FIG. 10.7. Progression Using Diminished 7 Chords

After you've taken some time to try out the many triad options to use for this progression, compare notes with the options below.

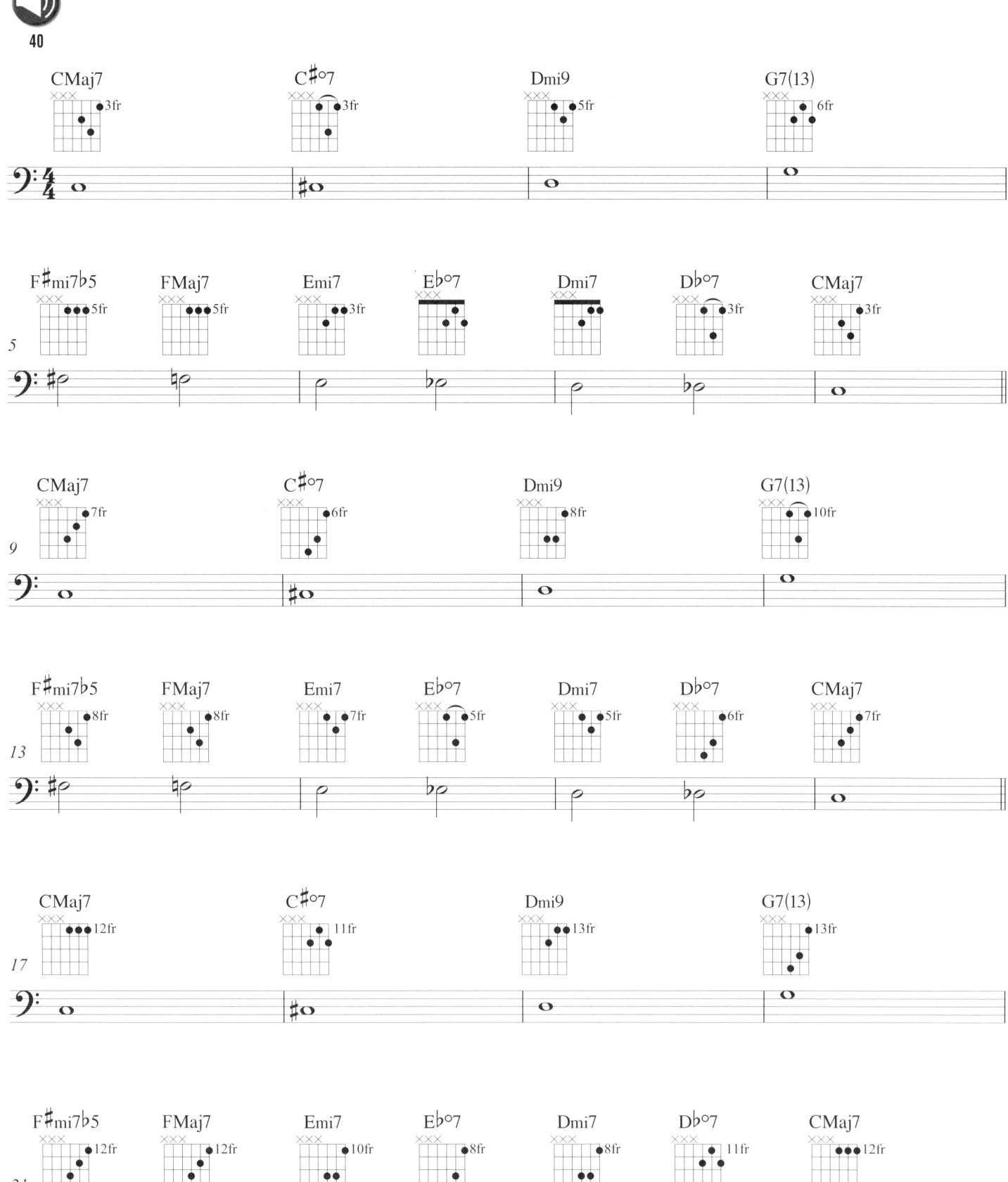

FIG. 10.8. Three Options for Mixed Chord Progression

CHAPTER 11

Minor-Major 7 Chords

Minor-major 7 chords are natural to melodic minor, harmonic minor, and harmonic major scales. Look at the make up of those three scales:

Melodic Minor

Harmonic Minor

Harmonic Major

FIG. 11.1. Three Scales: Melodic Minor, Harmonic Minor, Harmonic Major

Chapter 4 shows the triad make-up of each of these scales. Building seventh chords from each degree of these scales shows where the minor-major 7 chords fall.

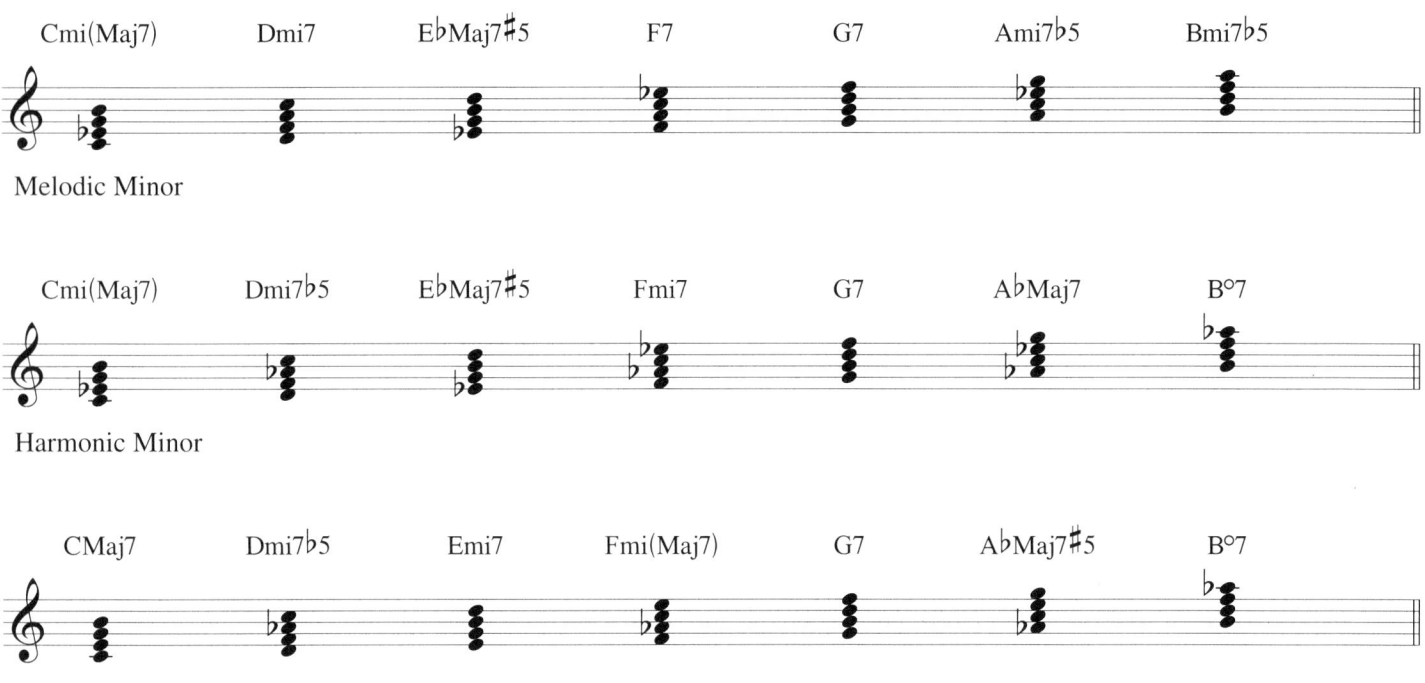

FIG. 11.2. Seventh Chords in Minor Scales

The I chord in melodic minor and harmonic minor scales is minor-major 7. The IV chord in harmonic major scales is minor-major 7.

A look at a Cmi(Maj7) chord reveals an E♭+ triad as its three high notes.

FIG. 11.3. Cmi(Maj7), E♭+

An E♭+ triad can be played starting on E♭, G, or B, using the same fingering for each inversion.

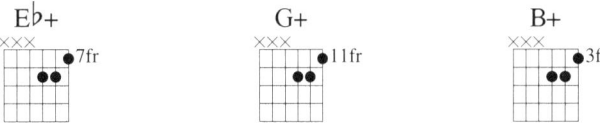

FIG. 11.4. E♭+, G+, B+

Seen this way, you can play an augmented triad starting on any chord tone of a minor-major 7 chord except for the root. That'll give you some mental flexibility in the way that you think of approaching these minor-major 7 chords and their associate augmented triads. However, you should continue to think of the high note as related to the seventh chord rather than the triad because it will be more helpful in landing on the needed seventh chord in time while playing a progression.

CHAPTER 11. Minor-Major 7 Chords (Miller)

Here is a reimagined blues using all minor-major 7 chords as an exercise. Try finding the augmented triads to use.

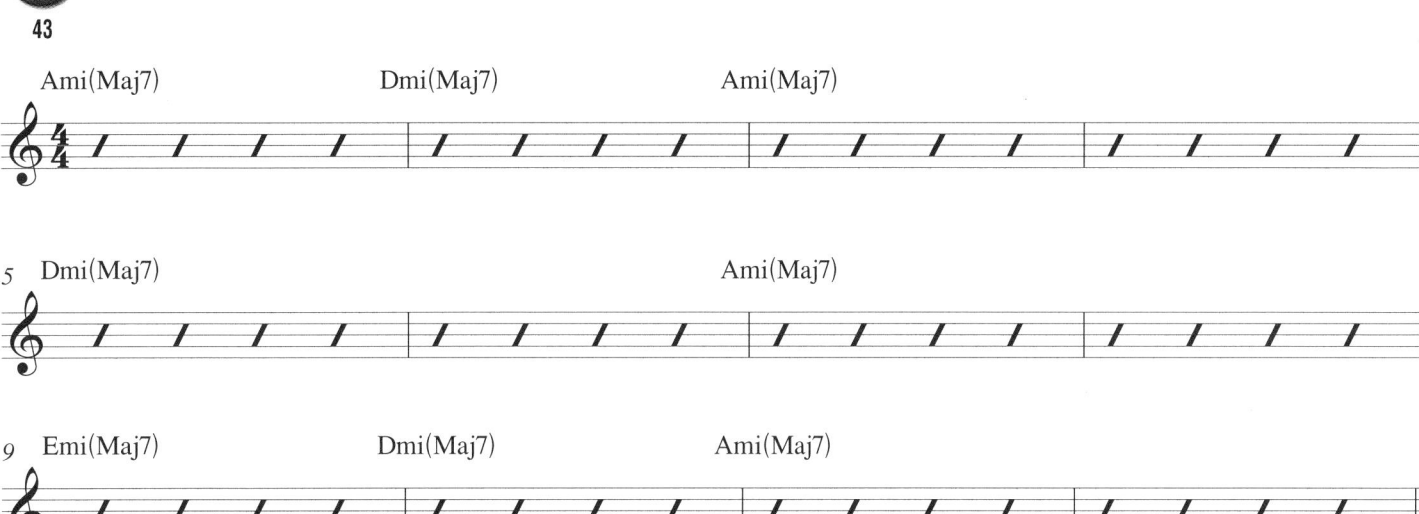

FIG. 11.5. 12-Bar Blues with Minor-Major 7 Chords

Now compare notes with these options for augmented triads. The first option starts with a C+ triad from the root and continues through, voice leading from there.

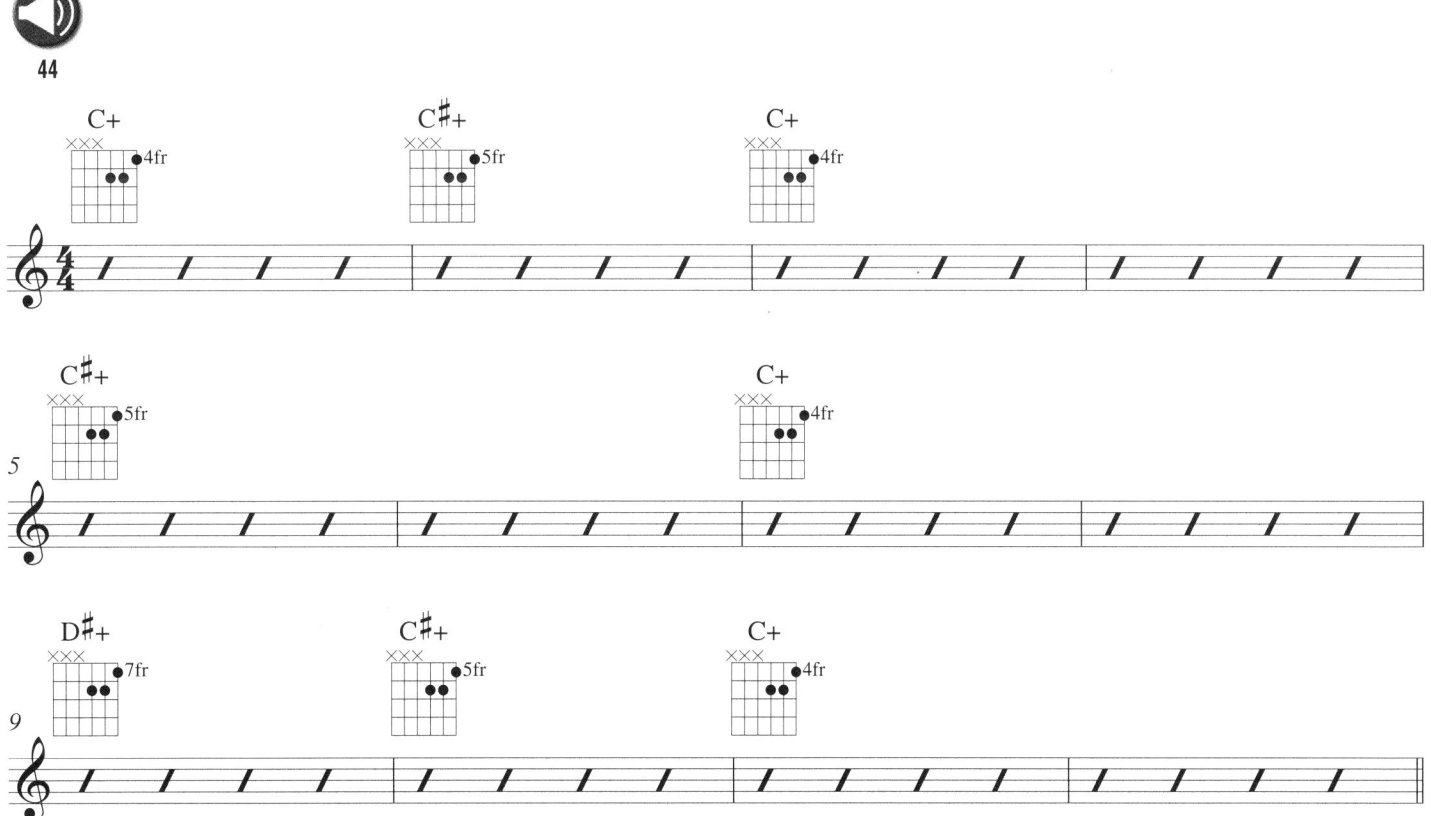

FIG. 11.6. Augmented Triads over Minor-Major Blues Option 1

Option 2 starts with E+ from the root. Since we know that C+ and E+ are the same triad (inversions of each other) they will both fit with the Ami(Maj7) in the first bar. Starting with E+ begins a new path to follow.

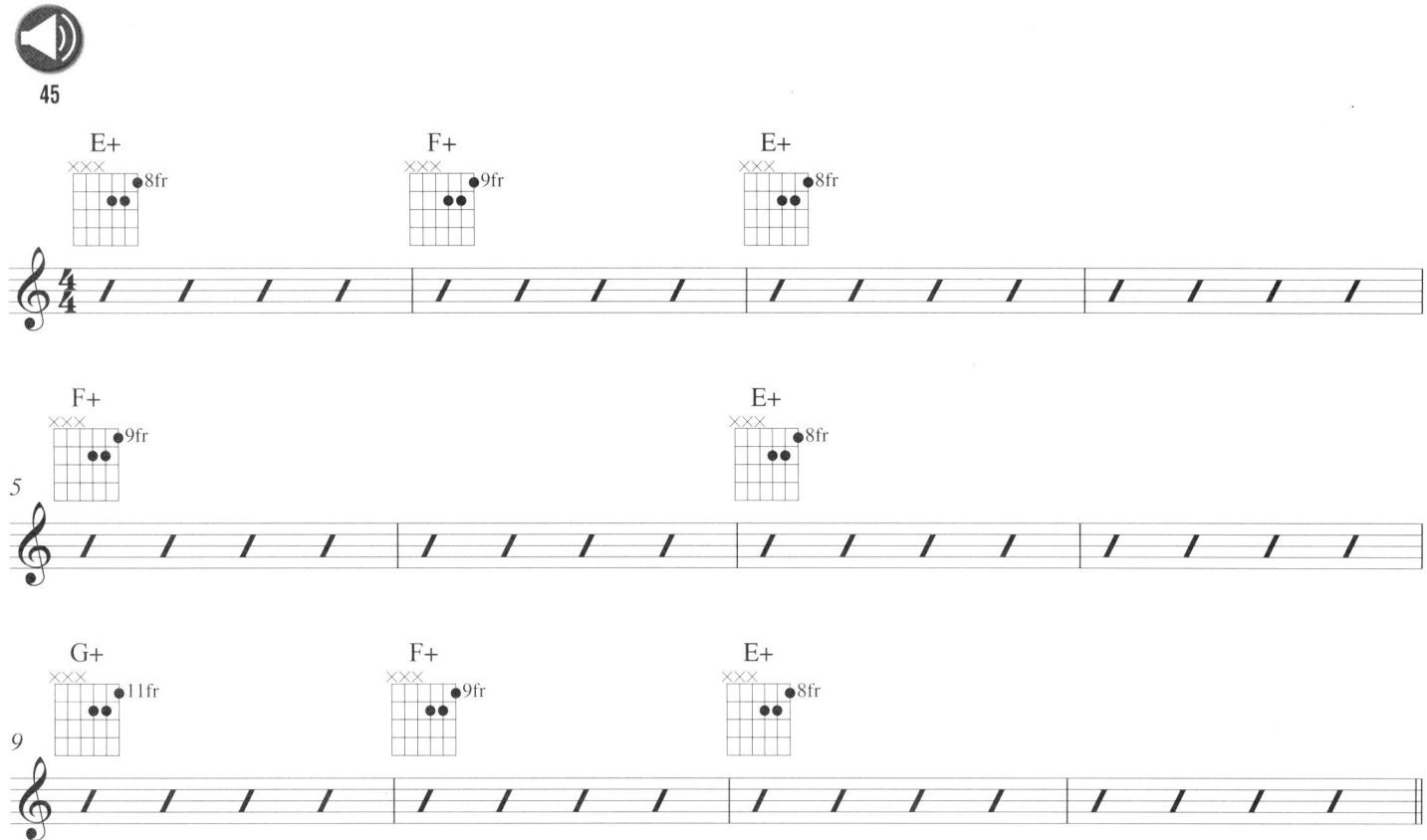

FIG. 11.7. Augmented Triads over Minor-Major Blues Option 2

For a third option, G♯+ is another inversion of the first two options: G♯+ = C+ and E+. Voice lead from there to get yet a new way through the progression.

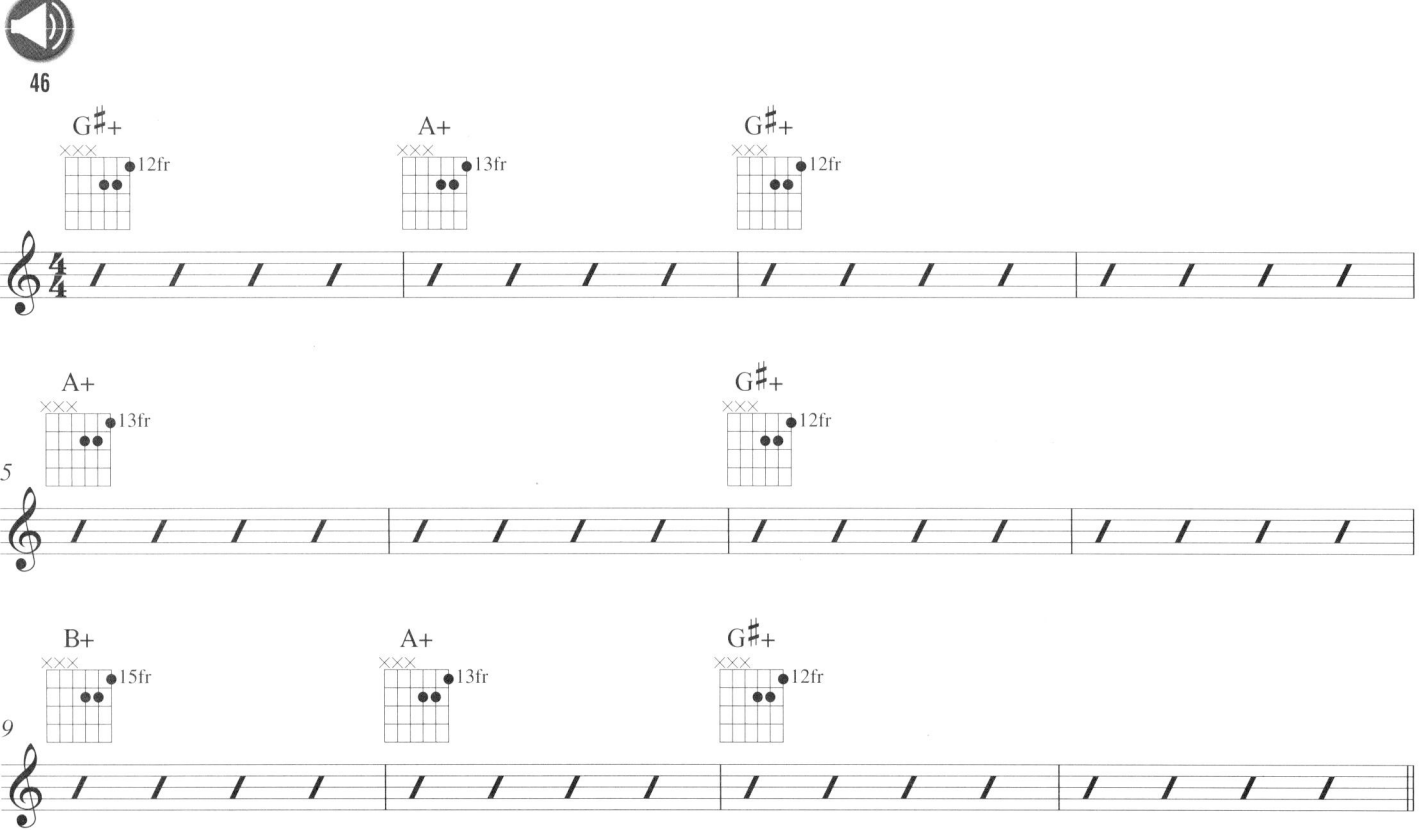

FIG. 11.8. Augmented Triads over Minor-Major Blues Option 3

CHAPTER 12

Matches and Deals: A Recap

As you've made your way through seventh chords, you might have noticed that some of them contain the same triad types in their top three notes. This means that you can organize the triads you play over seventh chords in a way that enables you to use the same chord forms in more than one context. It's a good deal! Efficient use of fingerings is ideal for guitarists. It promotes voice leading and smooth lines in improvising. Solving these sorts of match-game puzzles will help you to get around the fretboard in economic ways.

Here's the breakdown:

Triads	Their Uses
Major Triads	Major Triads, Minor 7 Chords
Minor Triads	Minor Triads, Major 7 Chords, Minor 7♭5 Chords
Diminished Triads	Diminished Triads, Dominant 7 Chords, Diminished 7 Chords
Augmented Triads	Augmented Triads, Minor-Major 7 Chords

Check out this progression:

FIG. 12.1. Progression to Voice Lead

Here's one way to play it in triad forms, which illustrates a particularly economical deal with voicings:

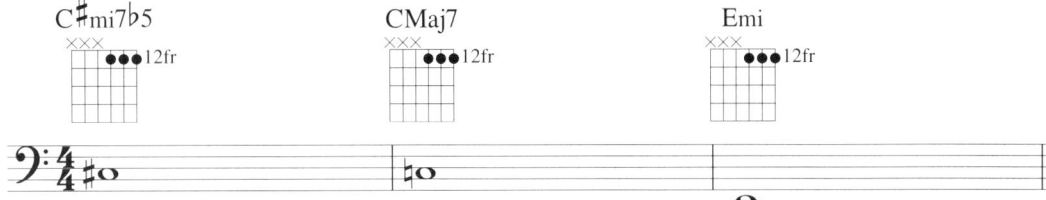

FIG. 12.2. Economic Voice Leading

In the above example, C♯mi7♭5 uses the ♭3 of the chord on top, CMaj7 uses the 3 on top, and Emi uses the root on top. You can't get more efficient than staying on the same chord throughout the progression! Be sure to listen to it in the context of the descending bass line to hear the chord changes in context. Make your own backing track with chords or bass lines, and have a listen to the ones provided, as well.

CHAPTER 13

Extensions and Natural Tensions

This system of playing triads over seventh chords can be thought of as putting the *upper structure triads* to use. More commonly, upper structure triads refer to triads superimposed on seventh chords with extensions or tensions, so there are more than four notes in the chord. For example, a CMaj9 = R 3 5 7 9 or C E G B D. The upper structure triad could be G rather than just thinking of the Emi as used in a CMaj7 chord without the added tension. It makes sense when you see the chord Emi7 on top of that CMaj9 chord. What triad would you use over an Emi7? G! The down side is that there is no E in a G triad, so there is no 3 of the C major included in the upper structure triad.

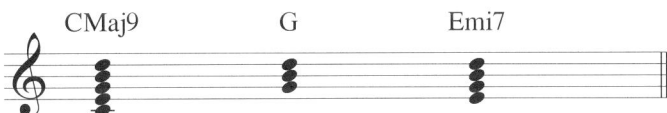

FIG. 13.1. CMaj9, G, Emi7

Making use of the upper structure triads in this way works once the chord tonality has been established. Additionally, if you think of this triad system as being a jumping off place from which to begin an improvised idea, you can then fill in other chord tones as you choose, or even other tensions.

Here are some upper structure triads contained in various quality seventh chords with tensions:

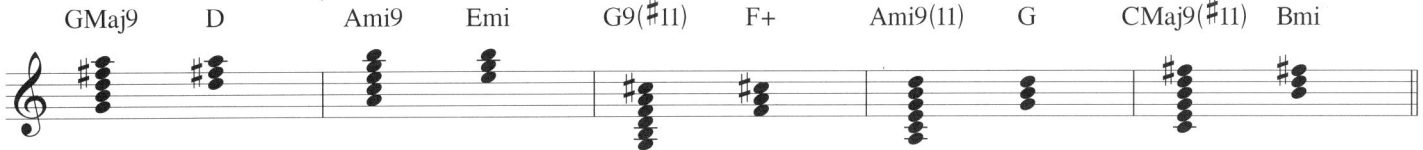

FIG. 13.2. Seventh Chords and their Upper Structure Triads

Combine the uppermost triads found in these extended seventh chords with some triad options found in the lower to middle voices of the chord for a more thorough working of the harmony. The following example shows different triads contained in seventh chords used within the harmonic rhythm of each chord.

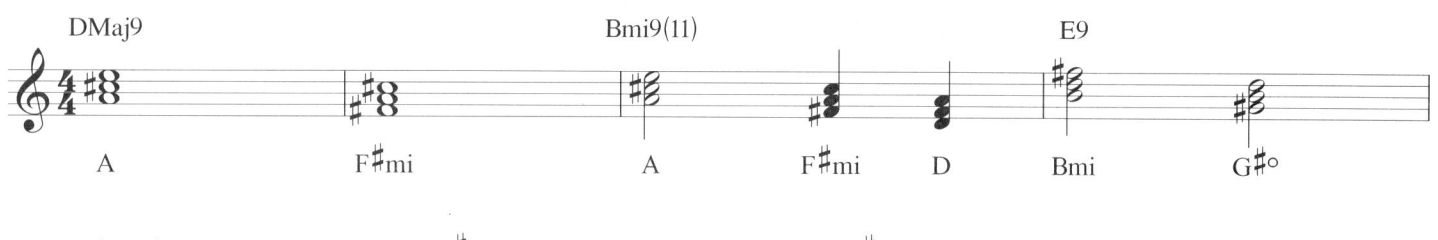

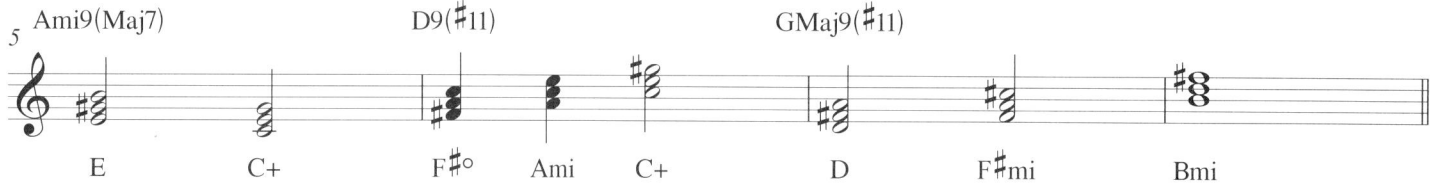

FIG. 13.3. Triads in Progression with Seventh Chords and Tensions

By mixing and matching the multiple triads found within the larger chords, you can eliminate any doubt about the chord quality that may linger if you only use the upper-most notes of the chord without, for example, the third of the chord. Factor in inversions of each triad in use and the possibilities increase.

Here is a voice-led option through the progression:

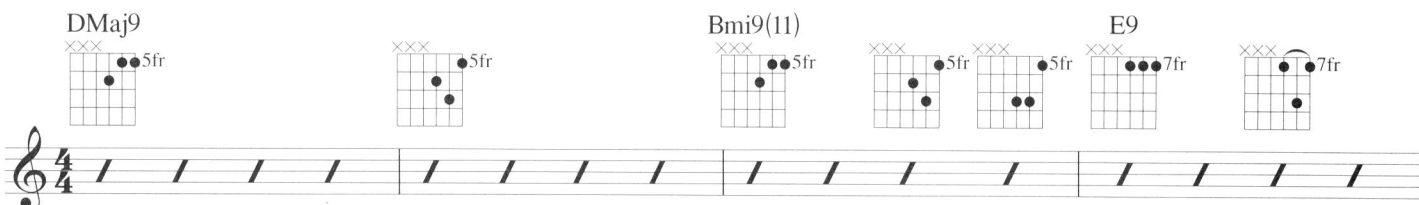

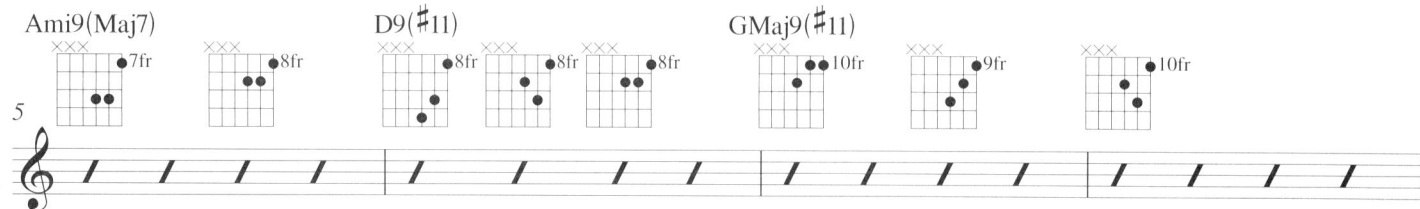

FIG. 13.4. Diagrams for Voice-Led Triads

CHAPTER 14

Altered Tensions

The upper structure of altered chords—seventh chords with altered tensions added to them—define the altered sound of the chord. When guitarists need to choose which notes of a five- or six-note chord will be played, since some will be necessarily sacrificed, triads can help to prioritize voicing decisions. In a bar of 4/4, there will be time to use two or more triad forms if a chord lasts for one measure. Comping decisions made in this way can be just as creative as single-note improvisation lines. In fact, in part III, you'll see how setting up these voicings will lead to improvised melodies.

FIG. 14.1. Triads in Altered Dominant Seventh Chords

Typically, altered dominant chords sound like they want to resolve to their I chord. Figure 14.2 shows some triad forms voice led through a progression featuring resolving altered dominant chords.

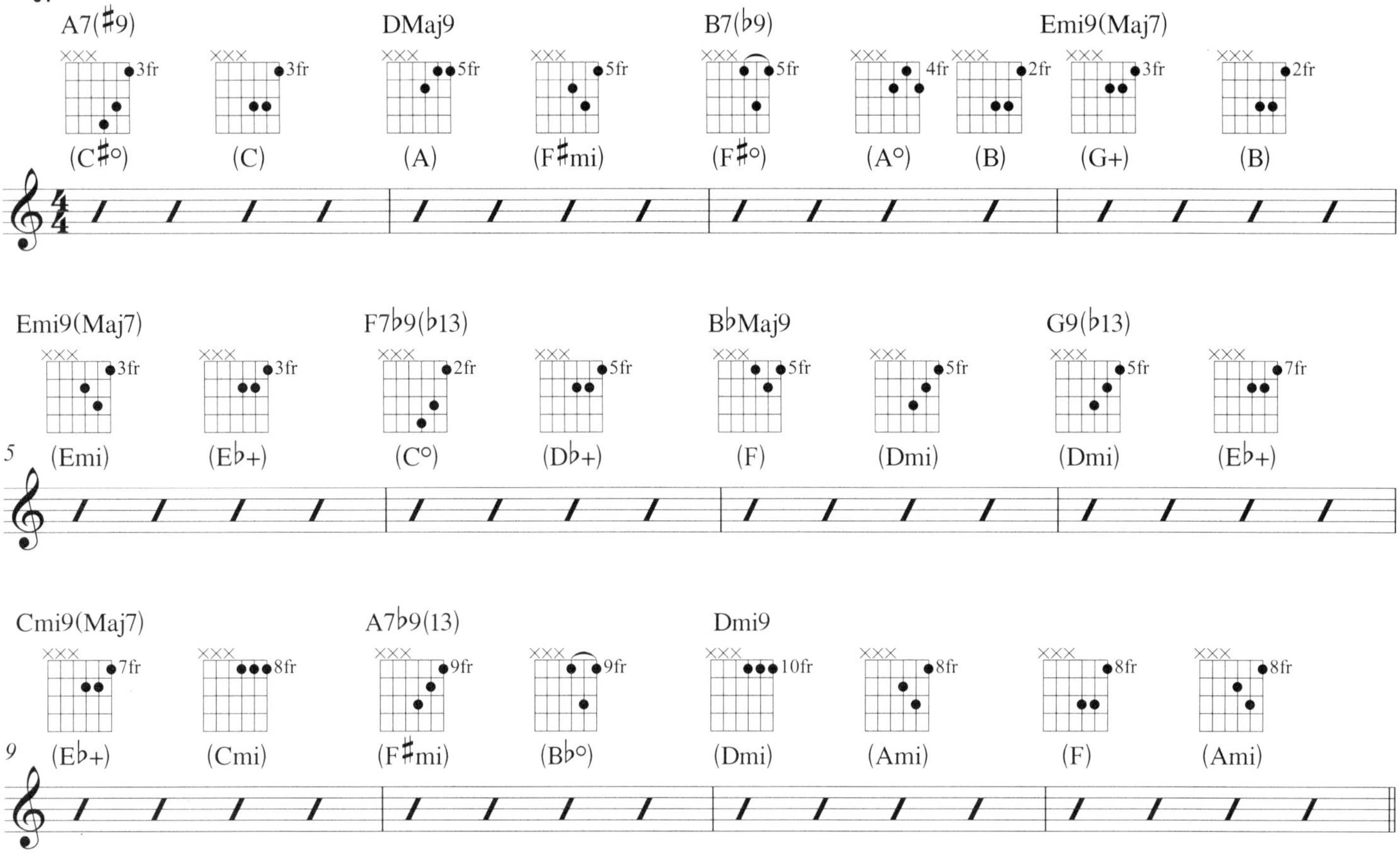

FIG. 14.2. Triads Used in Altered Dominant Chords

Now, revisit the habit of identifying the note that falls on the first E string. It will either be a chord tone or a tension of the seventh chord. Sketch it in to figure 14.2 and then compare with the answers below.

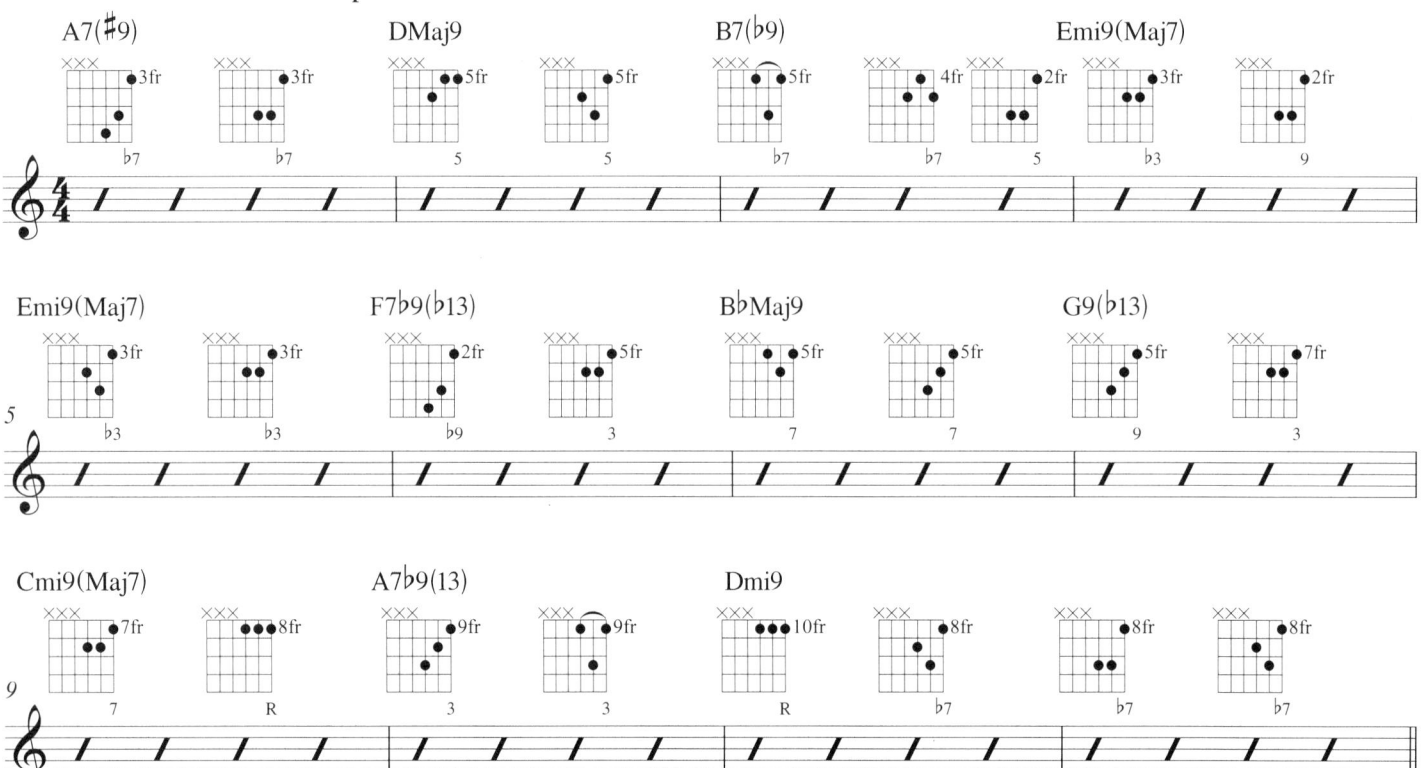

FIG. 14.3. Notes and Functions of Triads from 14.2

PART III
Comping and Soloing

CHAPTER 15

Comping

The following chord progressions are based on standard jazz repertoire. For practice, you can lay down a backing track of just a bass line if you'd like so that you can hear how effectively these three-string moveable chord forms will work without hearing any other comping. Additionally, go ahead and comp a backing track with chords that you might ordinarily use and then play the three-string moveable forms on top of that to hear how well the two chord approaches complement each other in the harmony.

To start the process, choose a triad form as a starting place to match the first chord in the progression. From there, the chord forms that follow will be dictated by what precedes them. As an exercise, write out the chord tone that falls on the first string for each of your choices. Triad choices and their chord tone identification on the first string will be shown on the pages following the initial chord chart for each chord progression. No specific tempo or groove is given so that you may feel free to mix it up!

Southern Charm

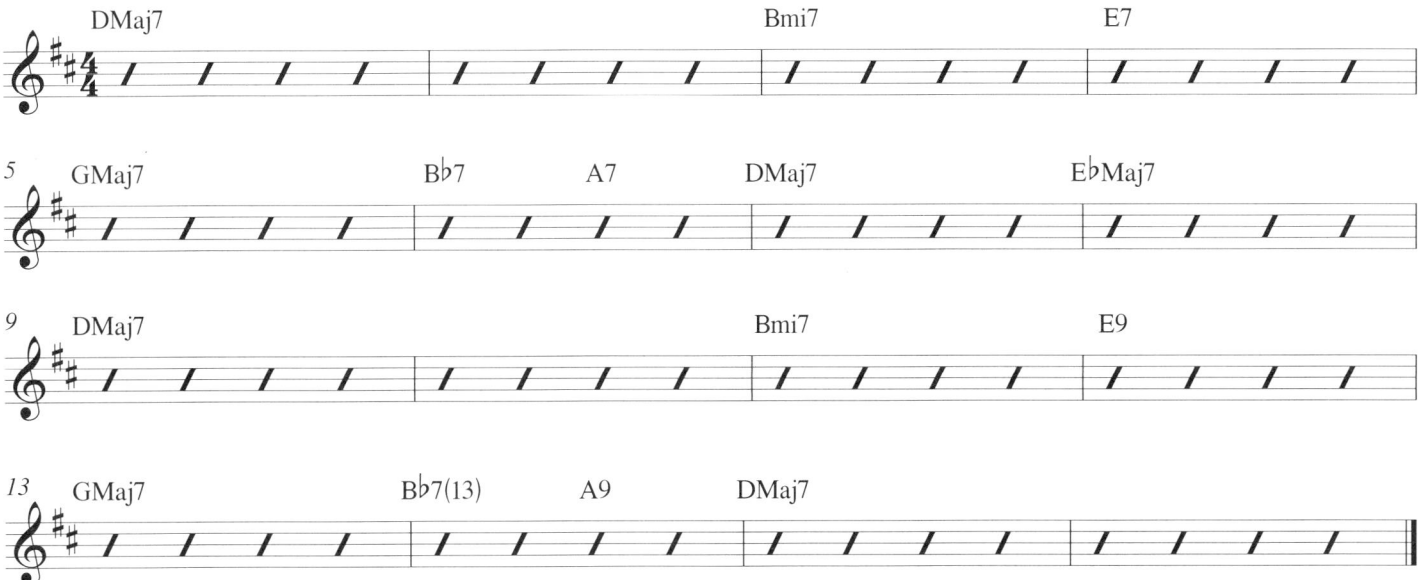

FIG. 15.1. Chord Progression to "Southern Charm"

Southern Charm

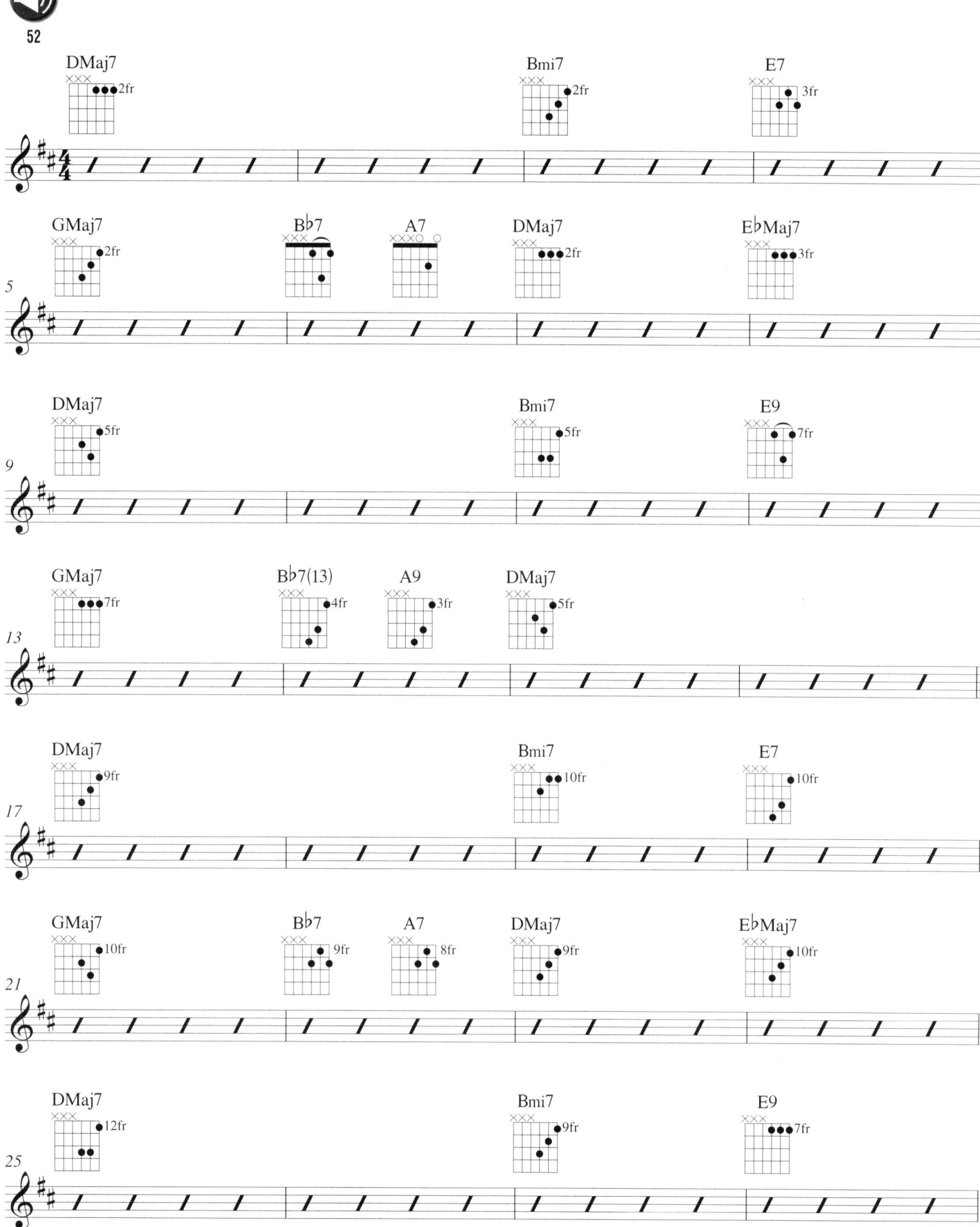

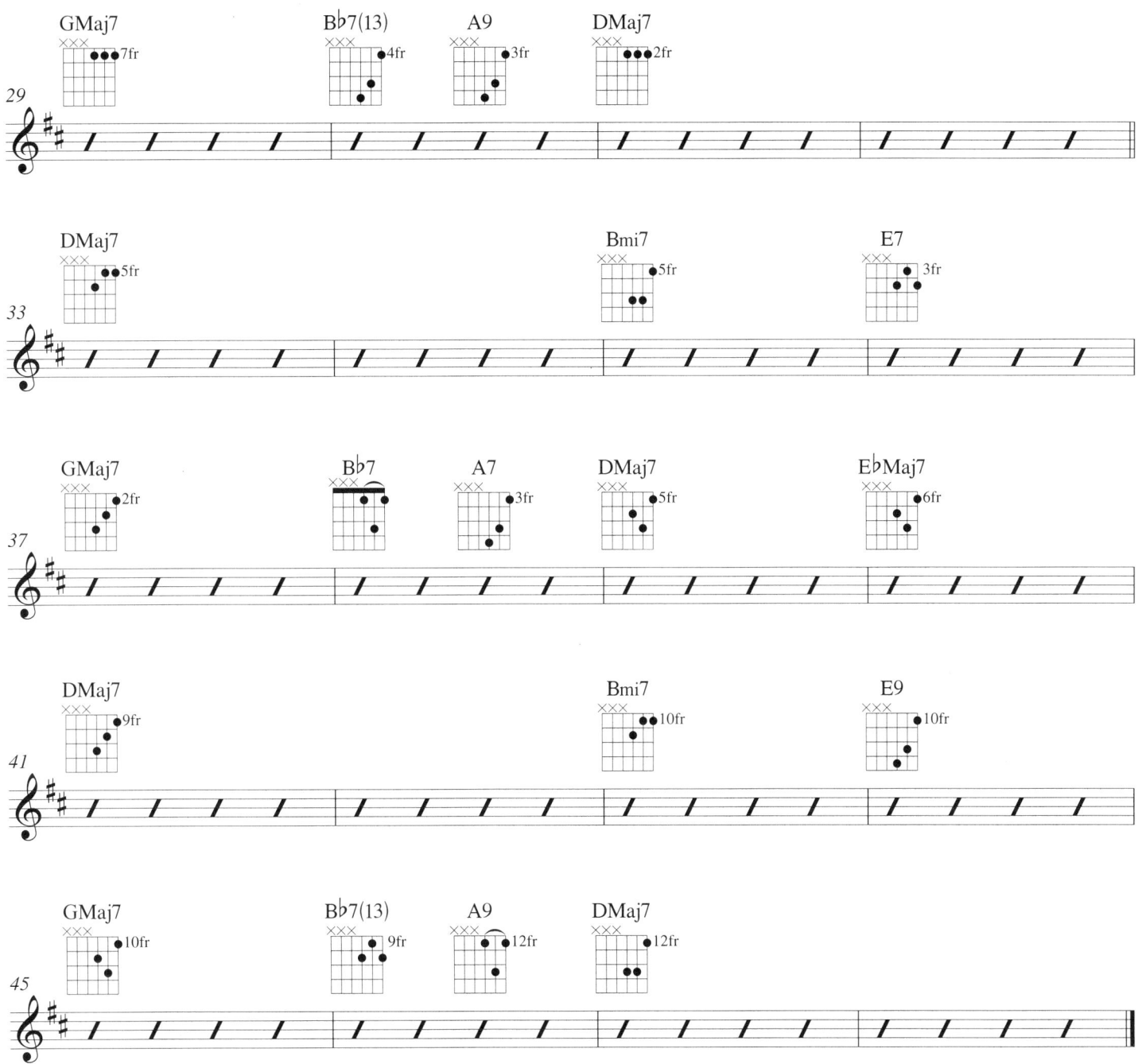

FIG. 15.2. Three Choruses of Triad Choices

Southern Charm

CHAPTER 15. Comping (Miller)

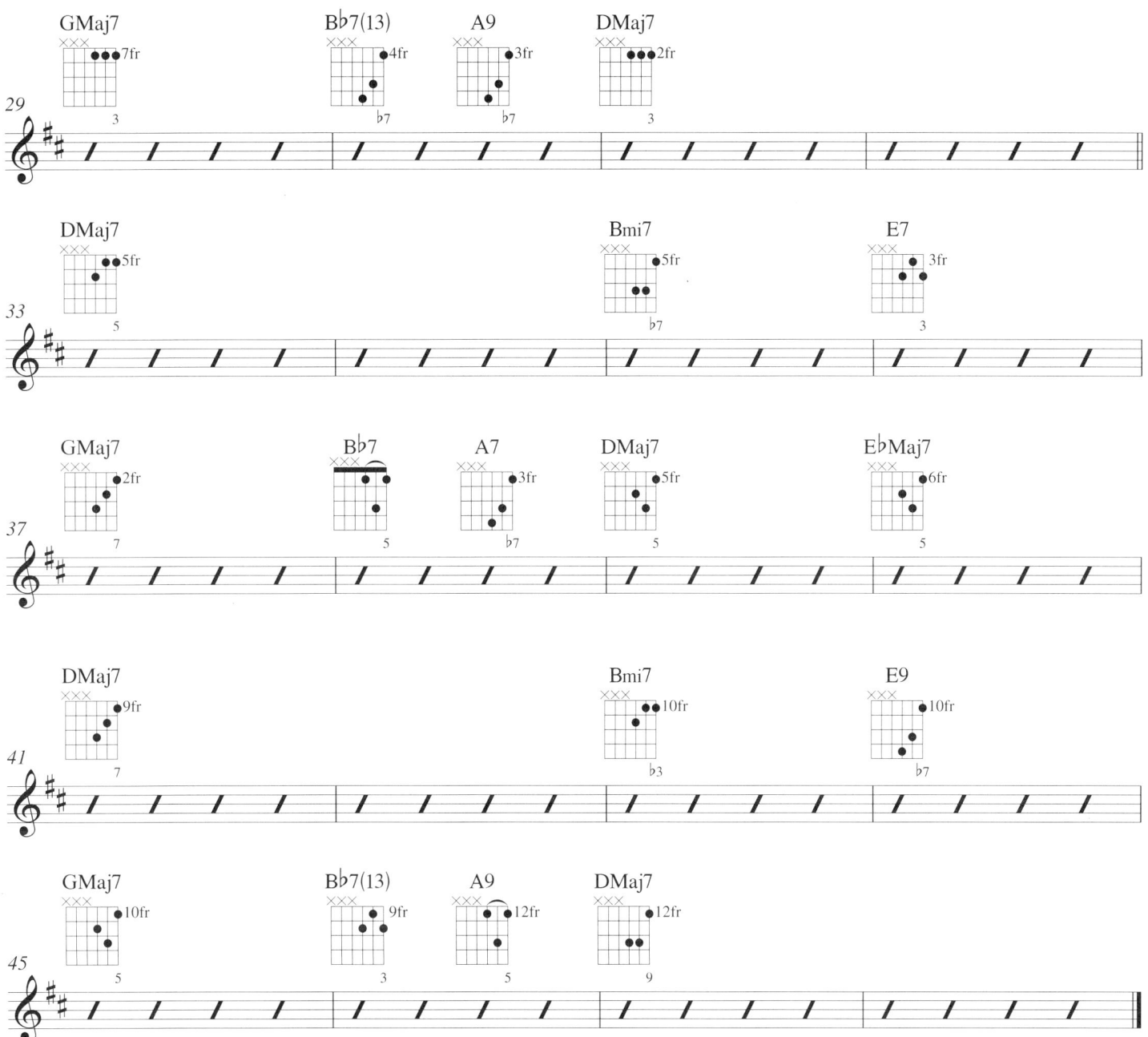

FIG. 15.3. Chord Tone I.D. for 15.2

My Roaming

FIG. 15.4. Chord Progression to "My Roaming"

My Roaming

53

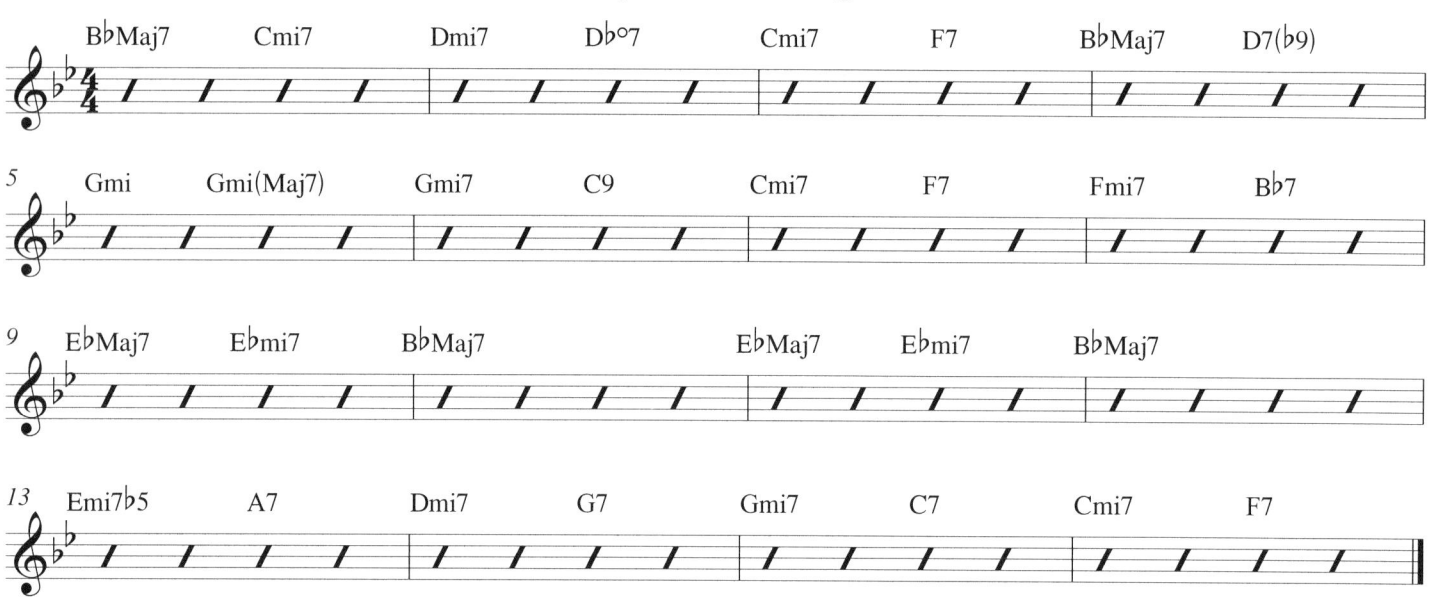

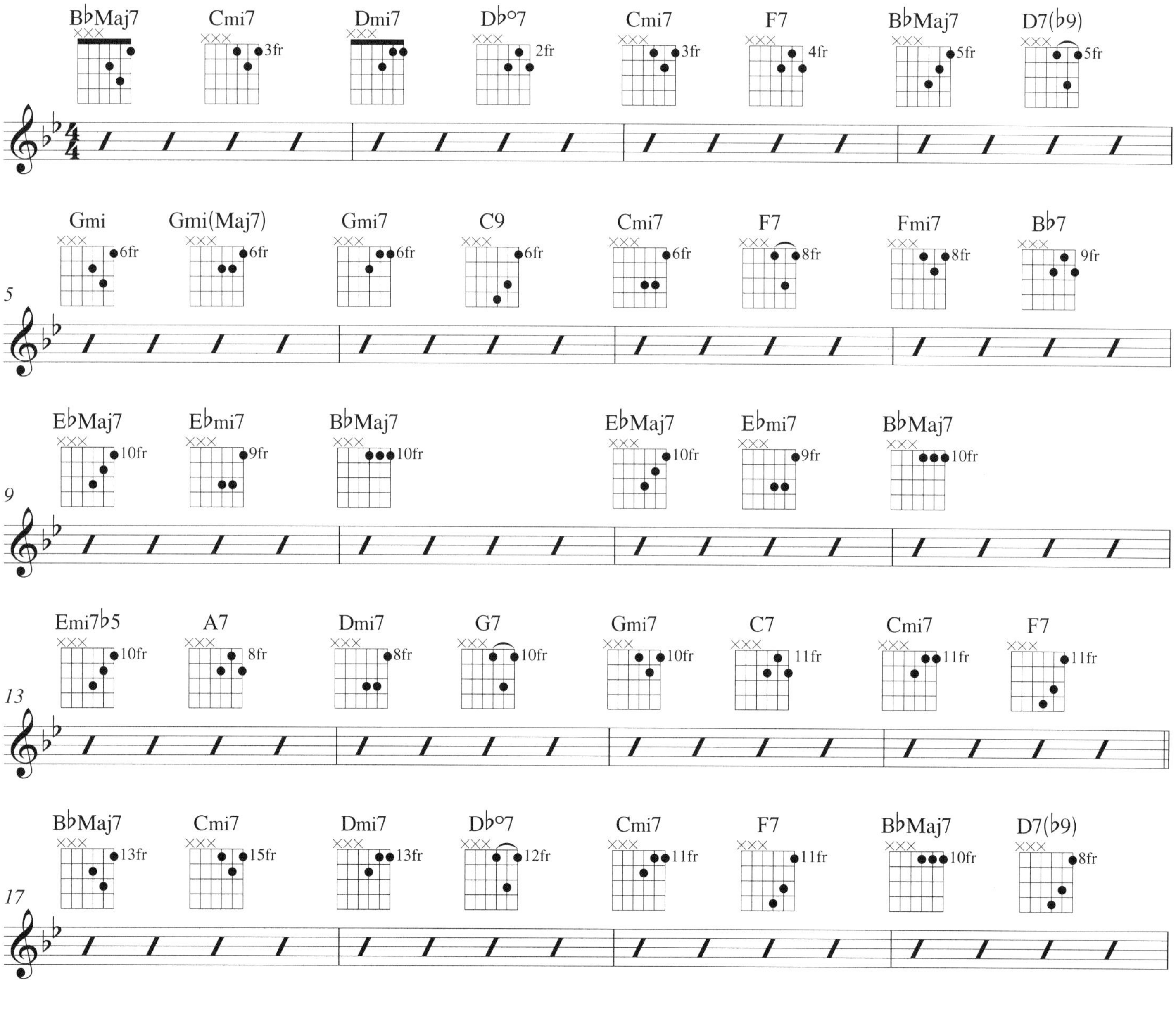

CHAPTER 15. Comping (Miller)

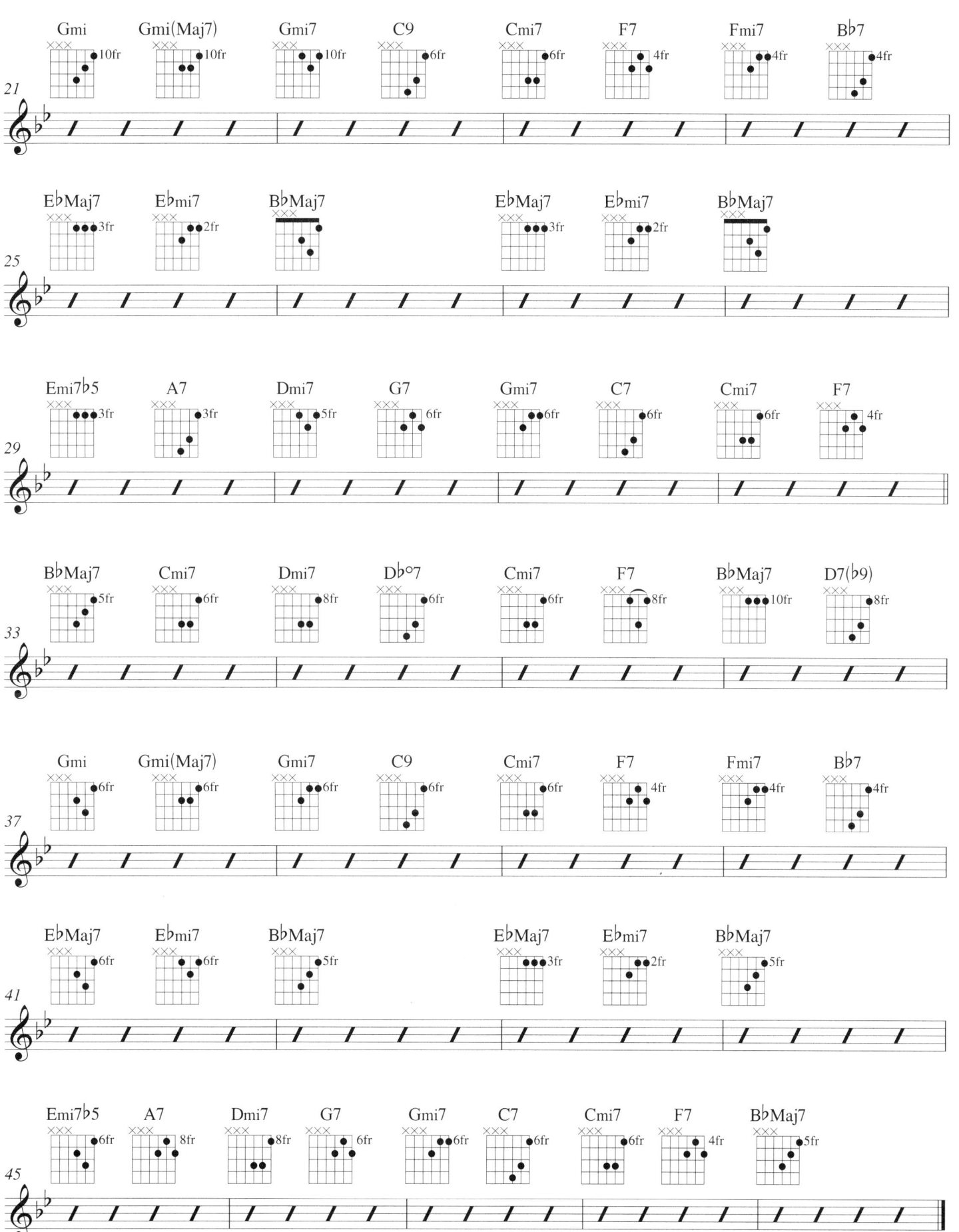

FIG. 15.5. Three Choruses of Triad Choices

My Roaming

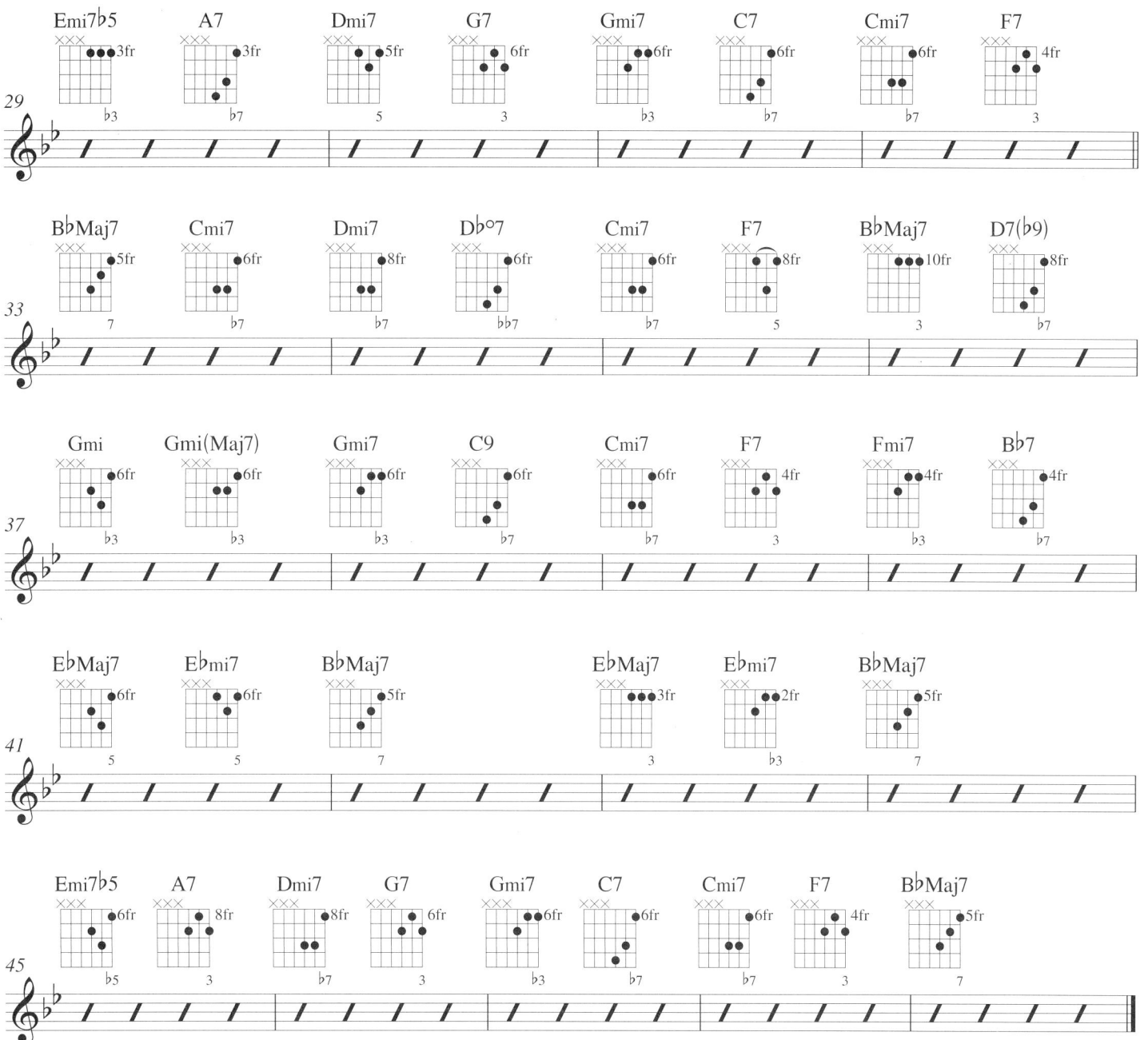

FIG. 15.6. Chord Tone I.D. for 15.5

Bonnie in Seoul

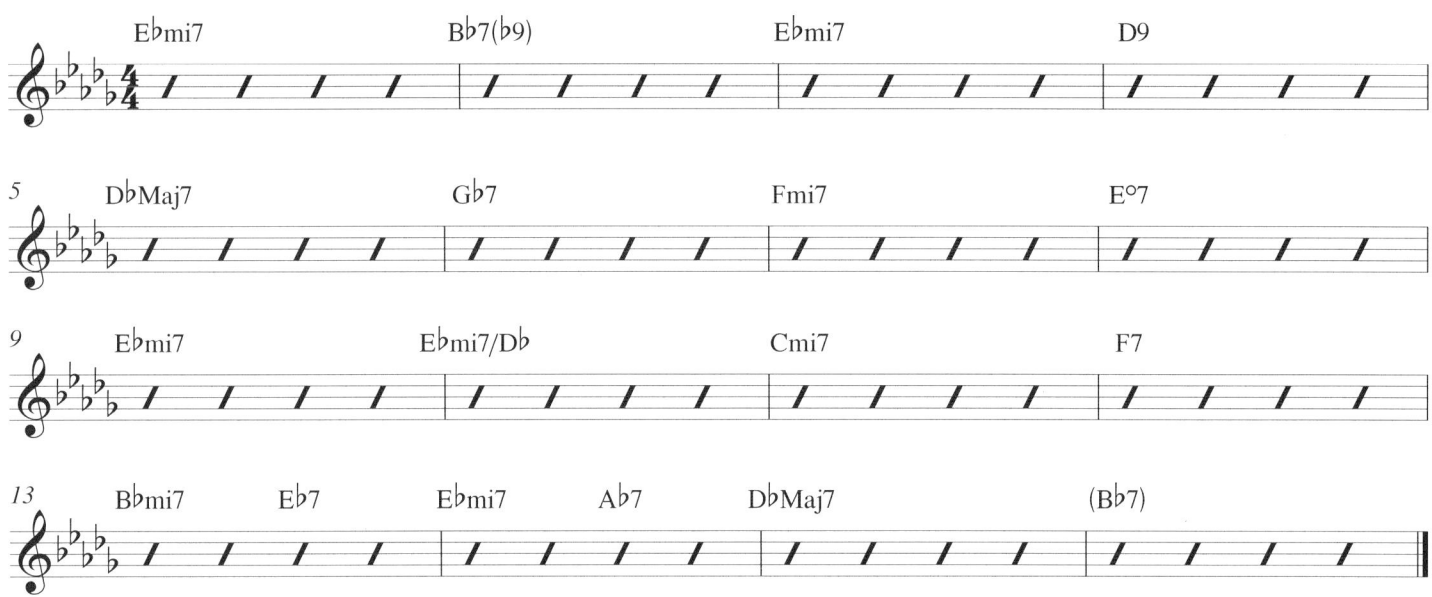

FIG. 15.7. Chord Progression to "Bonnie in Seoul"

Bonnie in Seoul

54

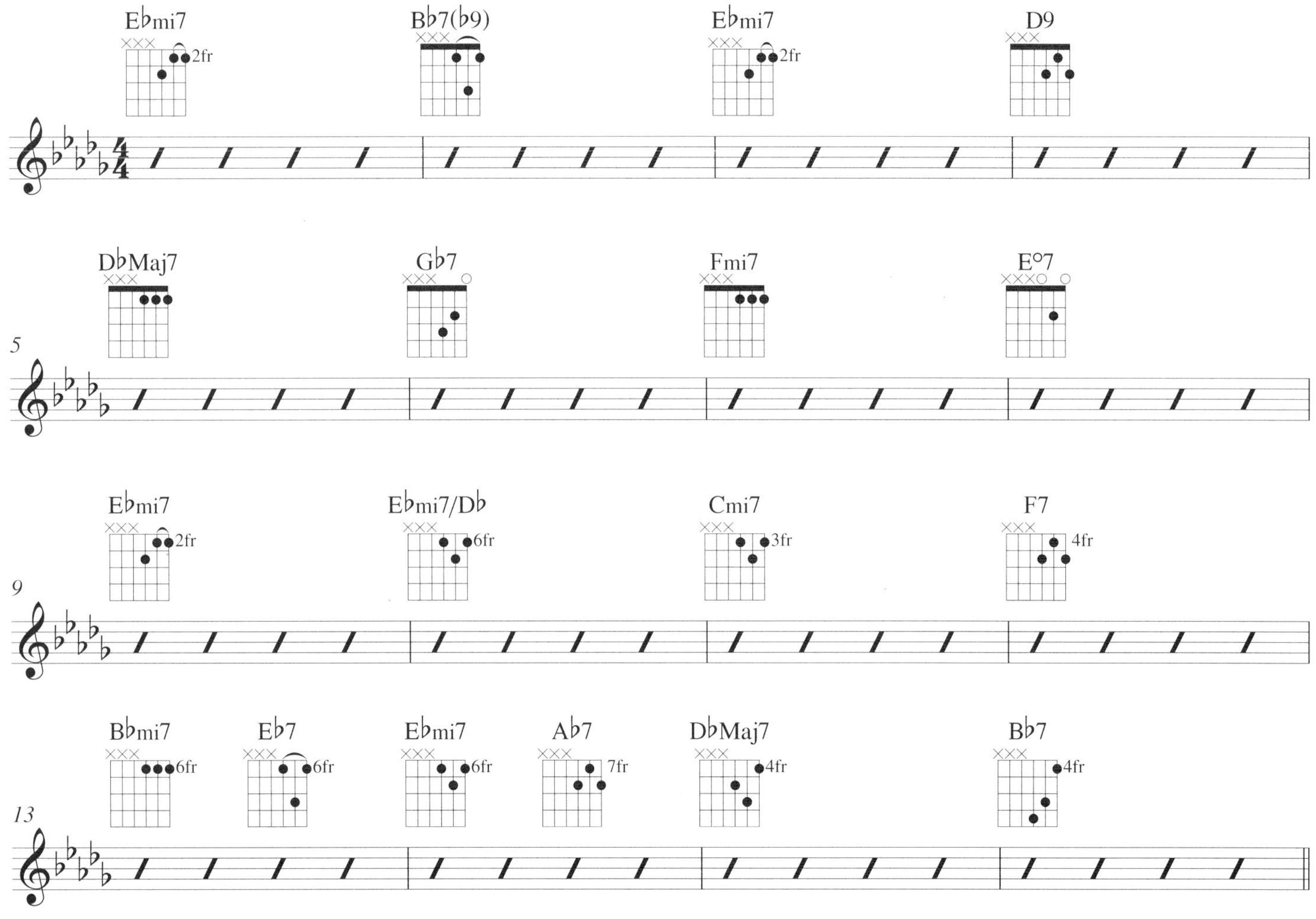

CHAPTER 15. Comping (Miller)

FIG. 15.8. Three Choruses of Triad Choices

Bonnie in Seoul

CHAPTER 15. Comping (Miller)

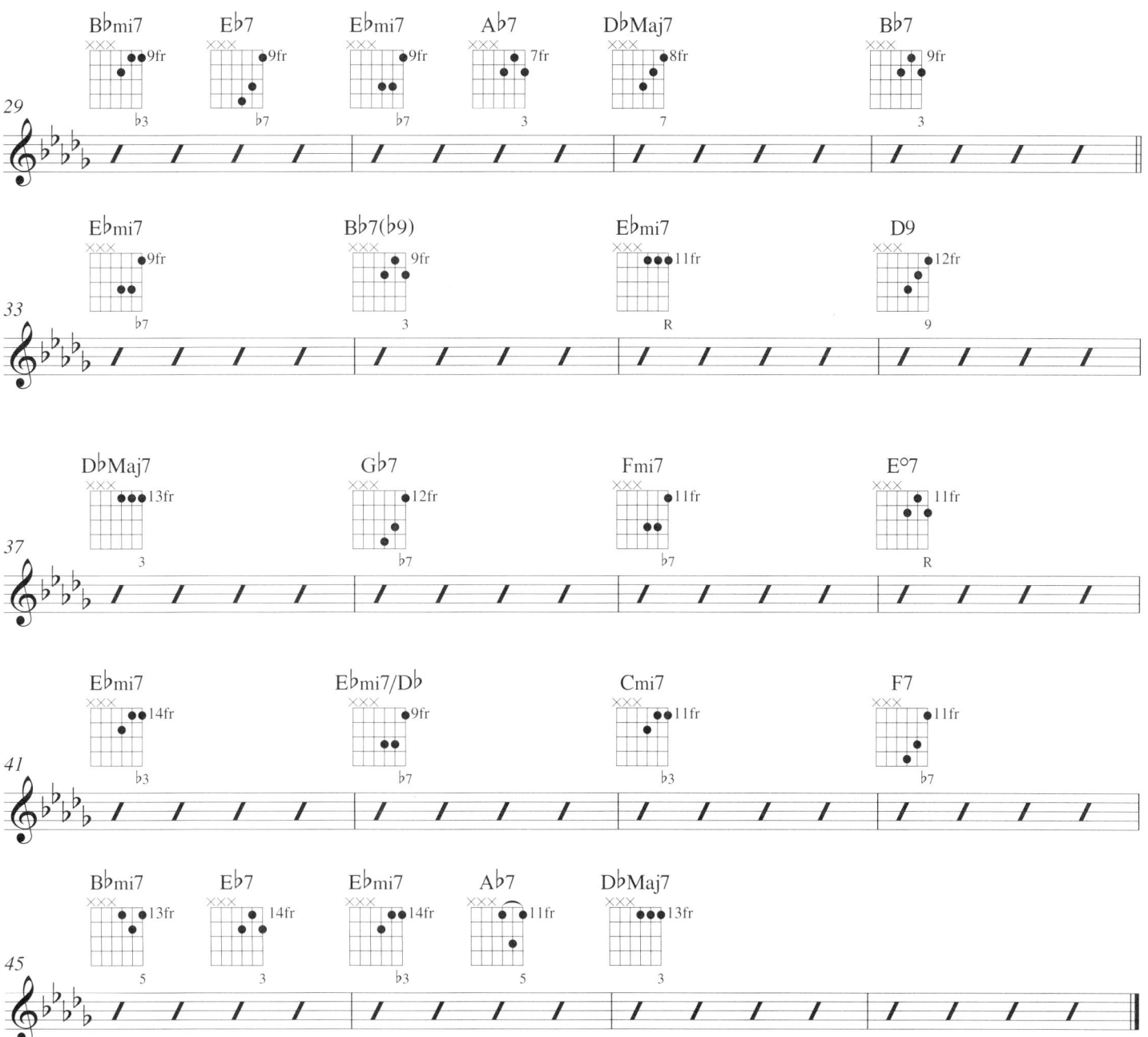

FIG. 15.9. Chord Tone I.D. for 15.8

CHAPTER 16

Soloing

In a sense, this chapter represents everything that the preceding chapters have been leading to and preparing you for. You've gained a new perspective and understanding of chords and the many places on the fretboard that they can be played. You're equipped with the mental practice of noticing what note falls on the first string and how you can use that information to identify chord shapes to place in an efficient way. You're connecting small chord shapes easily from one complex chord to another without being hindered by keys, scales, modes, or anything else that might have intimidated you before this perspective took hold. The next step to spring from all of this is to break up these triad forms into single-note lines.

Start right in with the examples from chapter 15. Simply play the notes on the first three strings separately. Repeat notes if you want to for rhythmic continuity; use any rhythms you'd like to fill out each measure. Notice the close connection from one chord to the next as you single out each of your chosen triad forms, which you are now thinking of as seventh chords.

Eventually, you'll be able to skip the step of writing out each three-string form as you begin to solo single note lines using the same voice led concepts. As you leave one chord and move to the next, you'll find yourself reaching for chord tones or tensions of the next chord just as you did when finding the triad forms. Having gone through the extensive practice and written exercise of economically working your way through each progression will make this part of your process easier and fun.

Let your ears be your guides as you add notes and phrases to the three string chord forms. Improvise! You will be making the changes already from simply breaking up the triad forms into single notes, but you'll notice that the shapes are becoming mental images rather than tightly held grips. In this way, you'll be more free to come and go from one chord to the next by visiting anything you'd like in between—including space! This process can relate to whatever you've worked on throughout your practice on the instrument. Ear training, scale practice, arpeggios, and patterns will all be useful to you as you find musical ways to thread lines through the juxtaposed chord forms that you've carefully and logically mapped out.

Again, keep in mind that the routine of sketching out each triad shape and making a note of how the chord tones relate to the seventh chord of the moment will become second nature as you turn the shapes into lines. You will still "see" the chords and visualize them as you navigate your way around the neck, but they will serve as interpreters, springboards, and guardrails for your ideas.

Mix these ideas together with anything else you might be working on. Let your mind's ear be your guide; that is the driving reason for improvising music. Your fingers will teach your ears new ideas, and your ears will begin to call for those ideas in new and interesting ways and musical contexts.

The songs here contain some passages that cannot rely on just knowing what key you're in and playing that scale. Having found the triad shapes for all of these chords grants you entry into soloing over the changes when you want to make an intelligent statement about the harmony on which the song is built.

Here are your blank canvases, also known as the chord charts from chapter 15, to improvise over using what you've investigated about them to this point. Use your backing tracks, your ears, and your mind's eye to solo using your now familiar places to start.

Take three choruses for each chord progression so that you can try out the different places to start: the inversions of the triads.

The second audio track of each pair can be heard as a demonstration improvisation on that progression.

Southern Charm

55, 56

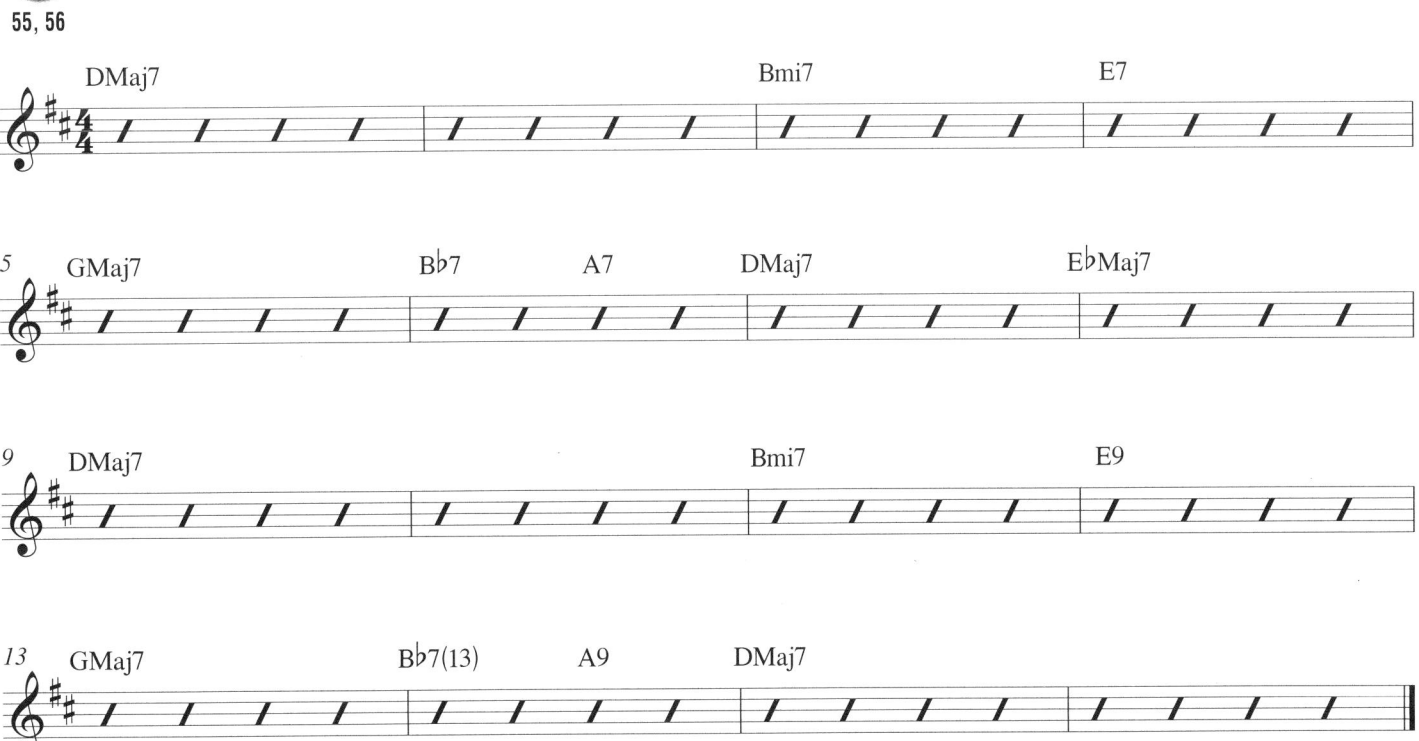

FIG. 16.1. "Southern Charm" Chord Chart

My Roaming

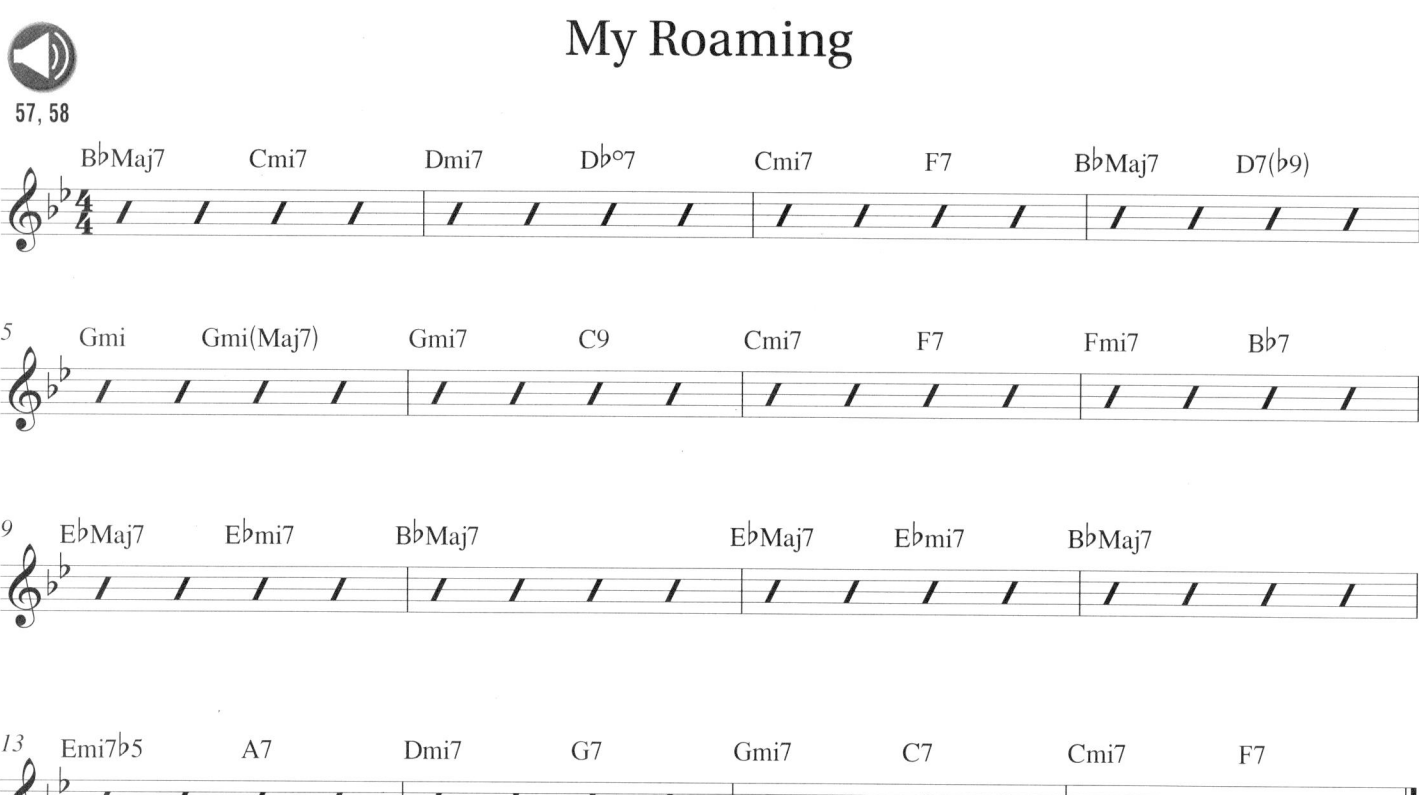

FIG. 16.2. "My Roaming" Chord Chart

Bonnie in Seoul

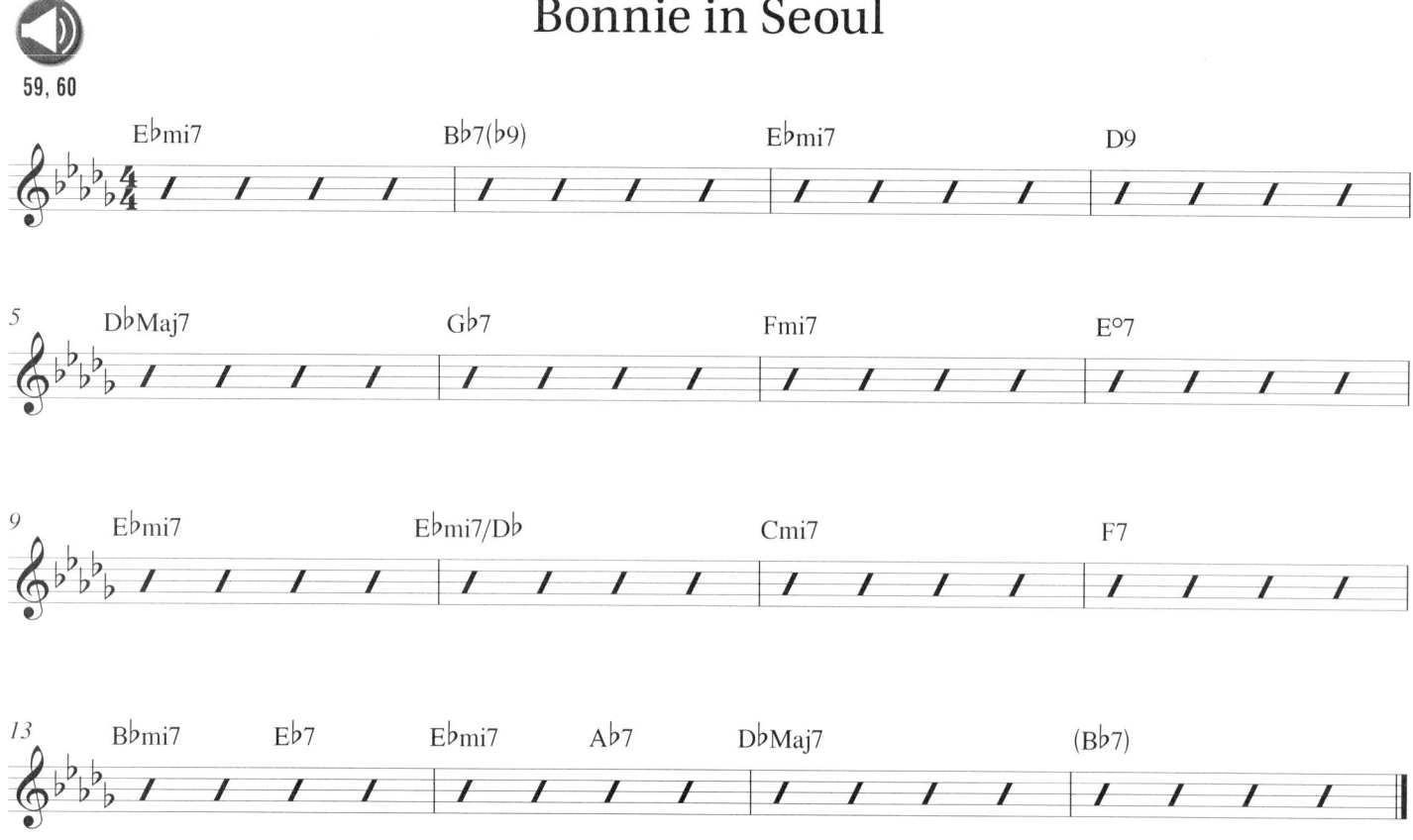

FIG. 16.3. "Bonnie in Seoul" Chord Chart

ABOUT THE AUTHOR

Photo by Emily Joy Ashman

Jane Miller is a professor in the Guitar Department at Berklee College of Music. She has presented master classes and performances around the world. With roots in both jazz and contemporary acoustic guitar, she performs solo guitar shows, plays with her group, and freelances with players in the New England Area. She is a composer and arranger, and has contributed many solo guitar arrangements to the Berklee Guitar Department library. She is a contributing editor for *Acoustic Guitar Magazine* and a former monthly columnist for *Premier Guitar Magazine* ("The Jazz Box"). She has recorded over seventy video lessons in jazz guitar for jamplay.com. Her newest recording *Boats* (her fifth CD) was released in April 2018 and contains fourteen of her compositions, which she arranged for her quartet featuring Tim Ray (piano), Lincoln Goines (bass), and Mark Walker (drums). Noted jazz writer Scott Yanow featured Jane in his book *The Great Jazz Guitarists: A Complete Guide*. In a review of Miller's 2013 solo recording *Three Sides to a Story*, Yanow called Miller "a fine guitarist whose attractive chord voicings and ability to swing at all tempos makes her a very complete musician... A flawless player...she is an important educator... Her playing, which sometimes recalls Joe Pass, makes the absence of a bassist and drummer barely noticeable."

janemillergroup.com

More Fine Publications

Berklee Press

GUITAR

BERKLEE ESSENTIAL GUITAR SONGBOOK
Kim Perlak, Sheryl Bailey, and Members of the Berklee Guitar Department Faculty
00350814 Book..........$22.99

BERKLEE GUITAR CHORD DICTIONARY
Rick Peckham
50449546 Jazz - Book..........$14.99
50449596 Rock - Book..........$12.99

BERKLEE GUITAR STYLE STUDIES
Jim Kelly
00200377 Book/Online Media..........$24.99

BERKLEE GUITAR THEORY
Kim Perlak and Members of the Berklee Guitar Department Faculty
00276326 Book..........$24.99

BLUES GUITAR TECHNIQUE
Michael Williams
50449623 Book/Online Audio..........$29.99

CLASSICAL TECHNIQUE FOR THE MODERN GUITARIST
Kim Perlak
00148781 Book/Online Audio..........$19.99

COUNTRY GUITAR STYLES
Mike Ihde
00254157 Book/Online Audio..........$24.99

CREATIVE CHORDAL HARMONY FOR GUITAR
Mick Goodrick and Tim Miller
50449613 Book/Online Audio..........$22.99

FUNK/R&B GUITAR
Thaddeus Hogarth
50449569 Book/Online Audio..........$19.99

GUITAR SWEEP PICKING
Joe Stump
00151223 Book/Online Audio..........$19.99

JAZZ GUITAR FRETBOARD NAVIGATION
Mark White
00154107 Book/Online Audio..........$22.99

MODAL VOICINGS FOR GUITAR
Rick Peckham
00151227 Book/Online Media..........$24.99

A MODERN METHOD FOR GUITAR – VOLUMES 1-3 COMPLETE*
William Leavitt
00292990 Book/Online Media..........$49.99
*Individual volumes, media options, and supporting songbooks available.

A MODERN METHOD FOR GUITAR SCALES
Larry Baione
00199318 Book..........$14.99

TRIADS FOR THE IMPROVISING GUITARIST
Jane Miller
00284857 Book/Online Audio..........$22.99

Berklee Press publications feature material developed at Berklee College of Music.
To browse the complete Berklee Press Catalog, go to
www.berkleepress.com

BASS

BERKLEE JAZZ BASS
Rich Appleman, Whit Browne & Bruce Gertz
50449636 Book/Online Audio..........$22.99

CHORD STUDIES FOR ELECTRIC BASS
Rich Appleman & Joseph Viola
50449750 Book..........$17.99

FINGERSTYLE FUNK BASS LINES
Joe Santerre
50449542 Book/Online Audio..........$24.99

FUNK BASS FILLS
Anthony Vitti
50449608 Book/Online Audio..........$22.99

INSTANT BASS
Danny Morris
50449502 Book/CD..........$9.99

METAL BASS LINES
David Marvuglio
00122465 Book/Online Audio..........$19.99

READING CONTEMPORARY ELECTRIC BASS
Rich Appleman
50449770 Book..........$22.99

PIANO/KEYBOARD

BERKLEE JAZZ KEYBOARD HARMONY
Suzanna Sifter
00138874 Book/Online Audio..........$29.99

BERKLEE JAZZ PIANO
Ray Santisi
50448047 Book/Online Audio..........$22.99

BERKLEE JAZZ STANDARDS FOR SOLO PIANO
Robert Christopherson, Hey Rim Jeon, Ross Ramsay, Tim Ray
00160482 Book/Online Audio..........$22.99

CHORD-SCALE IMPROVISATION FOR KEYBOARD
Ross Ramsay
50449597 Book/CD..........$19.99

CONTEMPORARY PIANO TECHNIQUE
Stephany Tiernan
50449545 Book/DVD..........$39.99

HAMMOND ORGAN COMPLETE
Dave Limina
00237801 Book/Online Audio..........$24.99

JAZZ PIANO COMPING
Suzanne Davis
50449614 Book/Online Audio..........$22.99

LATIN JAZZ PIANO IMPROVISATION
Rebecca Cline
50449649 Book/Online Audio..........$29.99

PIANO ESSENTIALS
Ross Ramsay
50448046 Book/Online Audio..........$26.99

SOLO JAZZ PIANO
Neil Olmstead
50449641 Book/Online Audio..........$42.99

DRUMS

BEGINNING DJEMBE
Michael Markus & Joe Galeota
00148210 Book/Online Video..........$16.99

BERKLEE JAZZ DRUMS
Casey Scheuerell
50449612 Book/Online Audio..........$26.99

DRUM SET WARM-UPS
Rod Morgenstein
50449465 Book..........$15.99

A MANUAL FOR THE MODERN DRUMMER
Alan Dawson & Don DeMichael
50449560 Book..........$14.99

MASTERING THE ART OF BRUSHES
Jon Hazilla
50449459 Book/Online Audio..........$19.99

PHRASING
Russ Gold
00120209 Book/Online Media..........$19.99

WORLD JAZZ DRUMMING
Mark Walker
50449568 Book/CD..........$27.99

BERKLEE PRACTICE METHOD

GET YOUR BAND TOGETHER
With additional volumes for other instruments, plus a teacher's guide.
Bass
Rich Appleman, John Repucci and the Berklee Faculty
50449427 Book/CD..........$24.99
Drum Set
Ron Savage, Casey Scheuerell and the Berklee Faculty
50449429 Book/CD..........$17.99
Guitar
Larry Baione and the Berklee Faculty
50449426 Book/CD..........$19.99
Keyboard
Russell Hoffmann, Paul Schmeling and the Berklee Faculty
50449428 Book/Online Audio..........$19.99

VOICE

BELTING
Jeannie Gagné
00124984 Book/Online Media..........$22.99

THE CONTEMPORARY SINGER
Anne Peckham
50449595 Book/Online Audio..........$29.99

JAZZ VOCAL IMPROVISATION
Mili Bermejo
00159290 Book/Online Audio..........$19.99

TIPS FOR SINGERS
Carolyn Wilkins
50449557 Book/CD..........$19.95

VOCAL WORKOUTS FOR THE CONTEMPORARY SINGER
Anne Peckham
50448044 Book/Online Audio..........$27.99

YOUR SINGING VOICE
Jeannie Gagné
50449619 Book/Online Audio..........$29.99

WOODWINDS & BRASS

TRUMPET SOUND EFFECTS
Craig Pederson & Ueli Dörig
00121626 Book/Online Audio.............$14.99

SAXOPHONE SOUND EFFECTS
Ueli Dörig
50449628 Book/Online Audio...........$17.99

THE TECHNIQUE OF THE FLUTE
Joseph Viola
00214012 Book...............................$19.99

STRINGS/ROOTS MUSIC

BERKLEE HARP
Felice Pomeranz
00144263 Book/Online Audio...........$24.99

BEYOND BLUEGRASS BANJO
Dave Hollander and Matt Glaser
50449610 Book/CD..........................$19.99

BEYOND BLUEGRASS MANDOLIN
John McGann and Matt Glaser
50449609 Book/CD..........................$19.99

BLUEGRASS FIDDLE & BEYOND
Matt Glaser
50449602 Book/CD..........................$19.99

CONTEMPORARY CELLO ETUDES
Mike Block
00159292 Book/Online Audio...........$24.99

EXPLORING CLASSICAL MANDOLIN
August Watters
00125040 Book/Online Media...........$24.99

THE IRISH CELLO BOOK
Liz Davis Maxfield
50449652 Book/Online Audio..........$27.99

JAZZ UKULELE
Abe Lagrimas, Jr.
00121624 Book/Online Audio............$24.99

MUSIC THEORY & EAR TRAINING

BEGINNING EAR TRAINING
Gilson Schachnik
50449548 Book/Online Audio...........$17.99

BERKLEE CONTEMPORARY MUSIC NOTATION
Jonathan Feist
00202547 Book...............................$24.99

BERKLEE MUSIC THEORY
Paul Schmeling
50449615 Book 1/Online Audio........$27.99
50449616 Book 2/Online Audio.......$24.99

CONTEMPORARY COUNTERPOINT
Beth Denisch
00147050 Book/Online Audio..........$24.99

MUSIC NOTATION
Mark McGrain
50449399 Book...............................$27.99
Matthew Nicholl & Richard Grudzinski
50449540 Book...............................$24.99

REHARMONIZATION TECHNIQUES
Randy Felts
50449496 Book...............................$29.99

CONDUCTING

CONDUCTING MUSIC TODAY
Bruce Hangen
00237719 Book/Online Media...........$24.99

MUSIC PRODUCTION & ENGINEERING

AUDIO MASTERING
Jonathan Wyner
50449581 Book/CD..........................$34.99

AUDIO POST PRODUCTION
Mark Cross
50449627 Book...............................$27.99

CREATING COMMERCIAL MUSIC
Peter Bell
00278535 Book/Online Media...........$19.99

HIP-HOP PRODUCTION
Prince Charles Alexander
50449582 Book/Online Audio..........$24.99

THE SINGER-SONGWRITER'S GUIDE TO RECORDING IN THE HOME STUDIO
Shane Adams
00148211 Book...............................$19.99

UNDERSTANDING AUDIO
Daniel M. Thompson
00148197 Book...............................$44.99

MUSIC BUSINESS

CROWDFUNDING FOR MUSICIANS
Laser Malena-Webber
00285092 Book...............................$17.99

ENGAGING THE CONCERT AUDIENCE
David Wallace
00244532 Book/Online Media..........$16.99

HOW TO GET A JOB IN THE MUSIC INDUSTRY
Keith Hatschek with Breanne Beseda
00130699 Book...............................$27.99

MAKING MUSIC MAKE MONEY
Eric Beall
00355740 Book...............................$29.99

MUSIC INDUSTRY FORMS
Jonathan Feist
00121814 Book...............................$17.99

MUSIC LAW IN THE DIGITAL AGE
Allen Bargfrede
00366048 Book...............................$24.99

MUSIC MARKETING
Mike King
50449588 Book...............................$24.99

PROJECT MANAGEMENT FOR MUSICIANS
Jonathan Feist
50449659 Book...............................$39.99

THE SELF-PROMOTING MUSICIAN
Peter Spellman
00119607 Book...............................$29.99

ARRANGING & IMPROVISATION

ARRANGING FOR HORNS
Jerry Gates
00121625 Book/Online Audio............$24.99

BERKLEE BOOK OF JAZZ HARMONY
Joe Mulholland & Tom Hojnacki
00113755 Book/Online Audio............$29.99

MODERN JAZZ VOICINGS
Ted Pease and Ken Pullig
50449485 Book/Online Audio..........$27.99

Prices subject to change without notice. Visit your local music dealer or bookstore, or go to www.berkleepress.com

SONGWRITING/COMPOSING

BEGINNING SONGWRITING
Andrea Stolpe with Jan Stolpe
00138503 Book/Online Audio...........$22.99

COMPLETE GUIDE TO FILM SCORING
Richard Davis
50449607 Book...............................$34.99

THE CRAFT OF SONGWRITING
Scarlet Keys
00159283 Book/Online Audio...........$24.99

CREATIVE STRATEGIES IN FILM SCORING
Ben Newhouse
00242911 Book/Online Media............$27.99

JAZZ COMPOSITION
Ted Pease
50448000 Book/Online Audio.......$39.99

MELODY IN SONGWRITING
Jack Perricone
50449419 Book...............................$26.99

MUSIC COMPOSITION FOR FILM AND TELEVISION
Lalo Schifrin
50449604 Book...............................$39.99

POPULAR LYRIC WRITING
Andrea Stolpe
50449553 Book...............................$17.99

THE SONGWRITER'S WORKSHOP
Jimmy Kachulis
Harmony
50449519 Book/Online Audio $29.99
Melody
50449518 Book/Online Audio $24.99

SONGWRITING: ESSENTIAL GUIDE
Pat Pattison
Lyric Form and Structure
50481582 Book...............................$19.99
Rhyming
00124366 Book...............................$22.99

SONGWRITING IN PRACTICE
Mark Simos
00244545 Book...............................$16.99

SONGWRITING STRATEGIES
Mark Simos
50449621 Book...............................$27.99

SONGBOOKS

NEW STANDARDS
Terri Lyne Carrington
00369515 Book...............................$29.99

WELLNESS/AUTOBIOGRAPHY

LEARNING TO LISTEN: THE JAZZ JOURNEY OF GARY BURTON
Gary Burton
00117798 Book...............................$34.99

MANAGE YOUR STRESS AND PAIN THROUGH MUSIC
Dr. Suzanne B. Hanser and
Dr. Susan E. Mandel
50449592 Book/Online Audio $34.99

MUSICIAN'S YOGA
Mia Olson
50449587 Book...............................$19.99

NEW MUSIC THERAPIST'S HANDBOOK
Dr. Suzanne B. Hanser
00279325 Book...............................$32.99

More Guitar Publications

    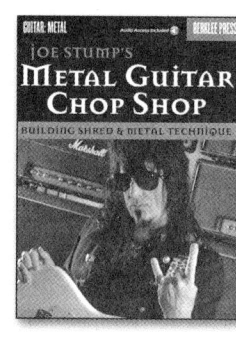 

ADVANCED READING STUDIES FOR GUITAR
William Leavitt
50449500 Book $19.99

BEBOP GUITAR SOLOS
Michael Kaplan
00121703 Book $16.99

BERKLEE BASIC GUITAR
William Leavitt
50449460 Phase 1 Book $12.99
50449470 Phase 2 Book $14.99

BERKLEE BLUES GUITAR SONGBOOK
Michael Williams
50449593 Book/Online Audio $27.99

BERKLEE ESSENTIAL GUITAR SONGBOOK
Kim Perlak, Sheryl Bailey, and Members of the Berklee Guitar Department Faculty
00350814 Book $19.99

BERKLEE GUITAR CHORD DICTIONARY
Rick Peckham
50449546 Book – Jazz $14.99
50449596 Book – Rock $12.99

BERKLEE GUITAR STYLE STUDIES
Jim Kelly
00200377 Book/Online Media $24.99

BERKLEE GUITAR THEORY
Kim Perlak and Members of the Berklee Guitar Department Faculty
00276326 Book $24.99

BERKLEE JAZZ STANDARDS FOR SOLO GUITAR
John Stein
50449653 Book/Online Audio $22.99

BERKLEE PRACTICE METHOD FOR GUITAR
Larry Baione
50449426 Book/CD $19.99

BERKLEE SOLO UKULELE
Karen Hogg
00327666 Book/Online Audio $16.99

BLUES GUITAR TECHNIQUE
Michael Williams
50449623 Book/Online Audio $29.99

THE CHORD FACTORY
Jon Damian
50449541 Book $27.99

CLASSICAL STUDIES FOR PICK-STYLE GUITAR
William Leavitt
50449440 Book $14.99

CLASSICAL TECHNIQUE FOR THE MODERN GUITARIST
Kim Perlak
00148781 Book/Online Audio $19.99

CONTEMPORARY JAZZ GUITAR SOLOS
Michael Kaplan
00143596 Book $16.99

COUNTRY GUITAR STYLES
Mike Ihde
00254157 Book/Online Audio $24.99

CREATIVE CHORDAL HARMONY FOR GUITAR
Mick Goodrick and Tim Miller
50449613 Book/Online Audio $22.99

FUNK/R&B GUITAR
Thaddeus Hogarth
50449569 Book/Online Audio $19.99

GUITAR SWEEP PICKING & ARPEGGIOS
Joe Stump
00151223 Book/Online Audio $19.99

THE GUITARIST'S GUIDE TO COMPOSING AND IMPROVISING
Jon Damian
50449497 Book/Online Audio $24.99

INTRODUCTION TO JAZZ GUITAR
Jane Miller
00125041 Book/Online Audio $22.99

JAZZ GUITAR FRETBOARD NAVIGATION
Mark White
00154107 Book/Online Audio $22.99

JAZZ GUITAR IMPROVISATION STRATEGIES
Steven Kirby
00274977 Book/Online Media $26.99

JAZZ IMPROVISATION FOR GUITAR
Garrison Fewell
50449594 Book/Online Audio – Harmonic Approach .. $29.99
50449503 Book/Online Audio – Melodic Approach $27.99

JAZZ SWING GUITAR
Jon Wheatley
00139935 Book/Online Audio $24.99

MELODIC RHYTHMS FOR GUITAR
William Leavitt
50449450 Book $17.99

Joe Stump's METAL GUITAR CHOP SHOP
50449601 Book/Online Audio $19.99

MODAL VOICING TECHNIQUES FOR GUITAR
Rick Peckham
00151227 Book/Online Video $24.99

A MODERN METHOD FOR GUITAR
William Leavitt
50449400 Volume 1 Book $15.99
50449404 Volume 1 Book/Online Audio $24.99
00137387 Volume 1 Book/Online Video $24.99
50449410 Volume 2 Book $16.99
50448021 Volume 2 Book/Online Audio $24.99
50449420 Volume 3 Book $19.99
00292989 Volume 3 Book/Online Audio $24.99
50449468 Volumes 1-3 Book $39.99
00292990 Volumes 1-3 Book/Online Media $49.99

A MODERN METHOD FOR GUITAR SCALES
Larry Baione
00199318 Book $14.99

A MODERN METHOD FOR GUITAR SONGBOOKS
50449539 Jazz with Online Audio $22.99
50449624 Rock with CD $17.99

PLAYING THE CHANGES: GUITAR
Mitch Seidman and Paul Del Nero
50449509 Book/CD $24.99

THE PRACTICAL JAZZ GUITARIST
Mark White
50449618 Book/Online Audio $27.99

THE PRIVATE GUITAR STUDIO HANDBOOK
Mike McAdam
00121641 Book $14.99

READING STUDIES FOR GUITAR
William Leavitt
50449490 Book $17.99

TRIADS FOR THE IMPROVISING GUITARIST
Jane Miller
00284857 Book/Online Audio $22.99

Visit your local music dealer or bookstore, or go to **www.berkleepress.com**
Prices and availability subject to change without notice

Berklee Press

DISTRIBUTED BY

Berklee Press

Your Source for Composing, Arranging & Conducting

ARRANGING FOR HORNS
by Jerry Gates
00121625 Book/Online Audio $22.99

ARRANGING FOR LARGE JAZZ ENSEMBLE
by Dick Lowell and Ken Pullig
50449528 Book/Online Audio $39.99

ARRANGING FOR STRINGS
by Mimi Rabson
00190207 Book/Online Audio $22.99

THE BERKLEE BOOK OF JAZZ HARMONY
by Joe Mulholland & Tom Hojnacki
00113755 Book/Online Audio $29.99

BERKLEE CONTEMPORARY MUSIC NOTATION
by Jonathan Feist
00202547 Book $24.99

BERKLEE MUSIC THEORY
by Paul Schmeling
Book 1: Basic Principles of Rhythm, Scales and Intervals
50449615 Book/Online Audio $24.99
Book 2: Fundamentals of Harmony
50449616 Book/Online Audio $24.99

COMPLETE GUIDE TO FILM SCORING
The Art and Business of Writing Music for Movies and TV
by Richard Davis
50449607 Book $34.99

CONDUCTING MUSIC TODAY
by Bruce Hangen
00237719 Book/Online Video $24.99

CONTEMPORARY COUNTERPOINT
Theory & Application
by Beth Denisch
00147050 Book/Online Audio $24.99

COUNTERPOINT IN JAZZ ARRANGING
by Bob Pilkington
00294301 Book/Online Audio $24.99

CREATING COMMERCIAL MUSIC
Advertising • Library Music • TV Themes
by Peter Bell
00278535 Book/Online Media $19.99

CREATIVE STRATEGIES IN FILM SCORING
by Ben Newhouse
00242911 Book/Online Media $27.99

JAZZ COMPOSITION
Theory and Practice
by Ted Pease
50448000 Book/Online Audio $39.99

JAZZ EXPRESSION
A Toolbox for Improvisation
with Larry Monroe
50448036 DVD $19.95

MODERN JAZZ VOICINGS
Arranging for Small and Medium Ensembles
by Ted Pease and Ken Pullig
50449485 Book/Online Audio $24.99

MUSIC COMPOSITION FOR FILM AND TELEVISION
by Lalo Schifrin
50449604 Book $39.99

MUSIC NOTATION
Theory & Technique for Music Notation
by Mark McGrain
50449399 Book $24.99

MUSIC NOTATION
Preparing Scores and Parts
by Matthew Nicholl and Richard Grudzinski
50449540 Book $24.99

REHARMONIZATION TECHNIQUES
by Randy Felts
50449496 Book $29.99

Berklee Press publications feature material developed at Berklee College of Music.

Visit your local music dealer or bookstore to order, or go to www.berkleepress.com

Prices, contents, and availability subject to change without notice.

More Great Books & Media from Berklee Press

DISTRIBUTED BY

Order these and hundreds more Berklee Press titles, including e-books, from your local music retailer at

halleonard.com

*All prices are listed in U.S. funds.
Prices, contents, and availability subject to change without notice.*

THE BERKLEE BOOK OF JAZZ HARMONY
Joe Mulholland & Tom Hojnacki
00113755 Book/Online Audio $29.99

BERKLEE ESSENTIAL GUITAR SONGBOOK
Kim Perlak, Sheryl Bailey, and Members of the Berklee Guitar Department Faculty
00350814 Book $19.99

BERKLEE JAZZ BASS
Rich Appleman, Bruce Gertz & Whit Browne
50449636 Book/Online Audio $22.99

BERKLEE JAZZ DRUMS
Casey Scheuerell
50449612 Book/Online Audio $24.99

BERKLEE JAZZ STANDARDS FOR SOLO PIANO
00160482 Book/Online Audio $22.99

BERKLEE MUSIC THEORY
Paul Schmeling
50449615 Book 1/Online Audio $27.99
50449616 Book 2/Online Audio $24.99

CONDUCTING MUSIC TODAY
Bruce Hangen
00237719 Book/Online Video $24.99

CONTEMPORARY COUNTERPOINT
Beth Denisch
00147050 Book/Online Audio $24.99

THE CONTEMPORARY SINGER
Anne Peckham
50449595 Book/Online Audio $29.99

THE CRAFT OF SONGWRITING
Scarlet Keys
00159283 Book/Online Audio $22.99

CREATING COMMERCIAL MUSIC
Peter Bell
00278535 Book/Online Media $19.99

CREATIVE STRATEGIES IN FILM SCORING
Ben Newhouse
00242911 Book/Online Media $27.99

CROWDFUNDING FOR MUSICIANS
Laser Malena-Webber
00285092 Book $17.99

HIP-HOP PRODUCTION
Prince Charles Alexander
50449582 Book/Online Media $24.99

A MODERN METHOD FOR GUITAR, VOLS. 1-3 COMPLETE
William Leavitt
00292990 Book/Online Media $49.99
50449468 Book Only $39.99
(Volumes 1-3 also available separately)

THE NEW MUSIC THERAPIST'S HANDBOOK
Suzanne B. Hanser
00279325 Book $32.99

NEW STANDARDS
Terri Lyne Carrington
00369515 Book $29.99

SONGWRITING: ESSENTIAL GUIDE
Pat Pattison
50481582 Lyric Form & Structure $19.99
00124366 Rhyming $22.99

UNDERSTANDING AUDIO
Daniel M. Thompson
00148197 Book $44.99

Berklee Online

Study Music Online with Berklee

Join a thriving online community and study Berklee's renowned curriculum in areas such as music production, songwriting, performance, and more!

- 200+ Courses
- Certificate Programs
- Bachelor's and Master's Degrees

online.berklee.edu | 1-866-BERKLEE |